Geographies of Media

Series Editors
Torsten Wissmann
Faculty of Architecture and Urban Planning
University of Applied Sciences
Erfurt, Germany

Joseph Palis
Department of Geography
University of the Philippines Diliman
Quezon, Philippines

Media is always spatial: spaces extend from all kinds of media, from newspaper columns to Facebook profiles, from global destination branding to individually experienced environments, and from classroom methods to GIS measurement techniques. Crucially, the way information is produced in an increasingly globalised world has resulted in the bridging of space between various scalar terrains. Being and engaging with media means being linked to people and places both within and beyond traditional political borders. As a result, media shapes and facilitates the formation of new geographies and other space-constituting and place-based configurations. The *Geographies of Media* series serves as a forum to engage with the shape-shifting dimensions of mediascapes from an array of methodological, critical and analytical perspectives. The series welcomes proposals for monographs and edited volumes exploring the cultural and social impact of multi-modal media on the creation of space, place, and everyday life.

Séverin Guillard • Joseph Palis
Ola Johansson
Editors

New Geographies of Music 2

Music in Urban Tourism, Heritage Politics, and Place-Making

Editors
Séverin Guillard
University of Picardie Jules Verne
Amiens, France

Ola Johansson
University of Pittsburgh at Johnstown
Johnstown, PA, USA

Joseph Palis
Department of Geography
University of the Philippines Diliman
Quezon, Philippines

ISSN 3005-012X ISSN 3005-0138 (electronic)
Geographies of Media
ISBN 978-981-97-2071-2 ISBN 978-981-97-2072-9 (eBook)
https://doi.org/10.1007/978-981-97-2072-9

© The Editor(s) (if applicable) and The Author(s), under exclusive license to Springer Nature Singapore Pte Ltd. 2024
This work is subject to copyright. All rights are solely and exclusively licensed by the Publisher, whether the whole or part of the material is concerned, specifically the rights of translation, reprinting, reuse of illustrations, recitation, broadcasting, reproduction on microfilms or in any other physical way, and transmission or information storage and retrieval, electronic adaptation, computer software, or by similar or dissimilar methodology now known or hereafter developed.
The use of general descriptive names, registered names, trademarks, service marks, etc. in this publication does not imply, even in the absence of a specific statement, that such names are exempt from the relevant protective laws and regulations and therefore free for general use.
The publisher, the authors and the editors are safe to assume that the advice and information in this book are believed to be true and accurate at the date of publication. Neither the publisher nor the authors or the editors give a warranty, expressed or implied, with respect to the material contained herein or for any errors or omissions that may have been made. The publisher remains neutral with regard to jurisdictional claims in published maps and institutional affiliations.

This Palgrave Macmillan imprint is published by the registered company Springer Nature Singapore Pte Ltd.
The registered company address is: 152 Beach Road, #21-01/04 Gateway East, Singapore 189721, Singapore

Paper in this product is recyclable.

SERIES EDITORS' PREFACE: THE SONG REMAINS THE SAME?

The second installment of the trilogy, *The New Geographies of Music*, returns with renewed vigor. After Matthew Hanchard's *Engaging with Digital Maps* (2024), this latest addition to our Geographies of Media series refocuses on music, echoing our beginnings in 2017.

In Boos' *Inhabiting Cyberspace and Emerging Cyberplaces*, we delved into the significance of practices for place-making, as he noted: "Communities are not necessarily connected to specific places but to issues that are important to their members. They create stories and histories around these topics" (2017, p. 30). This sentiment resonates in the current work, *Music in Urban Tourism, Heritage Politics, and Place-making* by Guillard, Johansson, and Palis. Through melody, rhythm, lyrics, and more, the music weaves narratives tied to place. While popular music production has become increasingly globalized (see Johansson, 2020), cities recognize and harness music as a cultural cornerstone, drawing tourists and attention to enhance both their visibility and municipal revenue. Artists and music itself are influenced by national hierarchies, city codes, and local regulations. If you haven't already, I invite you to explore the first part of the trilogy (Johansson et al., 2023), where you can delve deeper into topics such as the precarious work and life in the live music industry, an analysis of local scenes, national industry, and virtual platforms of French and American rap music, as well as the values of live music in urban development.

New Geographies of Music 2 offers an in-depth look into the consequences of heritage and place-making strategies as pivotal topics for discussion. As demonstrated by Ballico in Chap. 5, cities such as Nashville and Seattle leverage the value of their local music culture for tourism, even establishing dedicated museums. This raises questions about whether such musealization primarily aims to preserve and showcase local uniqueness and culture inherent to a specific place or if it also serves as a strategic marketing opportunity to position a city advantageously, potentially overlooking or underrepresenting certain music genres that may be considered "inconvenient." In Chap. 6, Bolderman clarifies that "music tourism can exacerbate racial inequality and social tension," as evidenced in the city of Austin (see O'Meara & Tretter, 2013; Wissmann, 2014).

Some places undeniably possess a strong connection to specific music genres, whether inherited by local musicians, constructed by the city's tourism industry, or ascribed through external stereotyping (see Wissmann, 2016). If you want to pick up the second book of our Geographies of Media series, *Sound, Space and Society*, you will find Peters exploring the interlinkage between place and music experience, using the example of a pirate radio ship. Peters' examination of intimate soundscapes highlights the impact of external sound sources on the listening experience, shaping atmospheric spaces of listening.

New Geographies of Music 2 not only delves deeper into the performative and place-making qualities of music, building upon the foundations laid by the first volume of the trilogy, but also offers an invaluable opportunity to explore the interplay of places and media more broadly. This renewed focus on the sonic medium aligns with the core premise of the book: "the importance of music to understand the spatial dimensions of society." Just as cities increasingly leverage music for marketing purposes, scholarly inquiry expands its scope to encompass a broader spectrum of media and place, moving beyond the visual realm. If Zonn finds that "watching movies is about place and experience" (2007, p. 64), we might want to add that listening to music is about place and experience as well.

Or, as Wim Wenders puts it: "[M]usic helped us to enter the city and find our way through it [...]."

Erfurt, Germany

Torsten Wissmann

REFERENCES

Boos, T. (2017). *Inhabiting cyberspace and emerging cyberplaces. The case of Siena, Italy.* Palgrave Macmillan.

Hanchard, M. (2024). *Engaging with digital maps. Our knowledgeable deferral to rough guides.* Palgrave Macmillan.

Johansson, O. (2020). *Songs from Sweden. Shaping pop culture in a globalized music industry.* Palgrave Macmillan.

Johansson, O., Guillard, S., & Palis, J. (2023). *New geographies of music 1. Urban policies, live music, and careers in a changing industry.* Palgrave Macmillan.

Peters, K. (2018). *Sound, space and society. Rebel radio.* Palgrave Macmillan.

Wissmann, T. (2014). *Geographies of urban sound.* Ashgate.

Wissmann, T. (2016). Lisbon story. Fado and the imaginative soundscape of the city in German cinema. In F. Velez de Castro & J. L. Fernandes (Eds.), *Territories of cinema: Representations of postmodernity* (pp. 123–162). Universidade de Málaga.

Zonn, L. (2007). Going to the movies: The filmic site as geographic endeavor. *Aether, 1,* 63–67.

CONTENTS

1 Introduction to the Spatiality of Popular Music: Music
Geographies, Urban Tourism, Heritage Policies, and
Place-making   1
Séverin Guillard, Ola Johansson, and Joseph Palis

2 Music in Surf Town Typology: Alternative Spaces of a
Subculture   21
Anne Barjolin-Smith

3 Street Piano: An Instrument of Urban Change   45
Alenka Barber-Kersovan

4 Tango Music: Between Heritage and Transnational
Resources. The Geographies of Tango In or From Buenos
Aires   73
Elsa Broclain, Francesca Cominelli, Sébastien Jacquot, and
Élodie Salin

5 Taking Music to the (Museum) Masses: Museum
Engagement with the Country and Grunge Music
Heritages of Nashville and Seattle   97
Christina Ballico

x CONTENTS

6 **The Hidden Music City: The Role of Music Tourism Imaginaries in the Regeneration of Detroit**   117
Leonieke Bolderman

Index   139

Notes on Contributors

Christina Ballico is a lecturer in the Department of Music at the University of Aberdeen, UK. She is the editor of *Geographically Isolated and Peripheral Music Scenes: Global Insights and Perspectives* (Palgrave, 2021) and the co-editor of *Music Cities: Evaluating a Global Cultural Policy Concept* (Palgrave, 2020).

Alenka Barber-Kersovan studied historical musicology, systematic musicology, psychology and aesthetics at the Universities of Ljubljana, Vienna and Hamburg and is currently teaching sociology of music at the Leuphana University in Lüneburg. She is engaged in the Urban Music Studies Scholars Network and is co-editing the publication series Urban Music Studies.

Anne Barjolin-Smith holds a Ph.D. in American Studies and dual Master's Degrees in Applied Linguistics and American Studies. She is an independent researcher who specializes in and actively participates in lifestyle sports. Barjolin-Smith is a certified English teacher at Florida Virtual School, Orlando, USA.

Leonieke Bolderman is Assistant Professor of Cultural Geography at the University of Groningen, The Netherlands. Her research concerns the role of art and culture in urban and regional development, specifically in relation to music, heritage, and tourism. Besides various research articles, she has written the monograph *Contemporary Music Tourism: A Theory of Musical Topophilia* (Routledge, 2020).

xii   NOTES ON CONTRIBUTORS

Elsa Broclain is an independent researcher based in Paris, France. She was formerly a Ph.D. candidate at the Research Center for Arts and Languages-École des Hautes Études en Sciences Sociales (CRAL-EHESS), and her research work focuses on heritage policies related to Tango in Buenos Aires. She now works at Films d'Ici, a film production company.

Francesca Cominelli is an associate professor at the University Paris 1 Panthéon-Sorbonne, France. She is a member of the Institute of Research and Higher Studies on Tourism (IREST) and directed from it 2017 to 2020. She is a member of EIREST and her work counts several collaborations with ICOMOS International, the Institute for French Savoir-Faire, the French Ministry of Culture, WIPO, the European Investment Bank, and OECD.

Séverin Guillard is Assistant Professor of Geography at the University of Picardie Jules Verne, Amiens, France, and a member of the research unit Habiter le Monde (Inhabiting the World). His research focuses on music, cultural policies, and events in French, American, and British cities.

Sébastien Jacquot is an assistant professor at the Paris 1 Panthéon-Sorbonne University, France, where he is a member of the research unit EIREST, and the director of Institute of Research and Higher Studies on Tourism (IREST).

Ola Johansson is Professor of Geography at the University of Pittsburgh, Johnstown, USA. He holds a Ph.D. from the University of Tennessee. Johansson is the author of the book *Songs from Sweden* (2020, Palgrave Macmillan), and co-author of *Sound, Society, and the Geography of Popular Music* and *World Regional Geography*.

Joseph Palis is an associate professor and chairperson in the Department of Geography at the University of the Philippines-Diliman, Philippines. He has been a DJ at WXYC-Chapel Hill since 2006.

Élodie Salin is Associate Professor of Geography, and a member of the research unit Espaces et Sociétés (ESO), at Le Mans University, France. She is also a member of EIREST at the Paris 1 Panthéon-Sorbonne University, and co-director of the Master's Degree in Territorial Management and Local Development at Le Mans University.

LIST OF FIGURES

Fig. 2.1   Cocoa Beach. (Source: Map by the author. Base map: Openstreetmap)   26

Fig. 2.2   Downtown Cocoa Beach. (Source: Map by the author. Base map: Openstreetmap)   27

Fig. 2.3   Sonny's Porch Concert. View from the street. Passersby. (Source: Photography taken by the author)   34

Fig. 5.1   Downtown Nashville Music Landmarks. (Source: Map by the author. Base map: openstreetmap)   105

Fig. 5.2   Downtown Seattle Music and Arts Landmarks. (Source: Map by the author. Base map: Openstreetmap)   108

CHAPTER 1

Introduction to the Spatiality of Popular Music: Music Geographies, Urban Tourism, Heritage Policies, and Place-making

Séverin Guillard, Ola Johansson, and Joseph Palis

Abstract Over the last few decades, a rich body of literature has explored the importance of music to understand the spatial dimensions of society. These geographic approaches to music are varied, depending on the background of the researchers. While music has generated a substantial interest among geographers, scholars in other disciplines have also developed related spatial perspectives on music. These multiple approaches to the

S. Guillard (✉)
University of Picardie Jules Verne, Amiens, France
e-mail: severin.guillard@u-picardie.fr

O. Johansson
University of Pittsburgh at Johnstown, Johnstown, PA, USA
e-mail: johans@pitt.edu

J. Palis
Department of Geography, University of the Philippines Diliman, Quezon, Philippines
e-mail: jepalis@up.edu.ph

© The Author(s), under exclusive license to Springer Nature Singapore Pte Ltd. 2024
S. Guillard et al. (eds.), *New Geographies of Music 2*, Geographies of Media, https://doi.org/10.1007/978-981-97-2072-9_1

1

geographies of popular music are the ones that our book series bring together. This volume is the second installment of a three-part book series, *New Geographies of Music*. In this chapter, we will explore these perspectives and discuss how they provide a multitude of lenses through which we can study popular music. Then, we will highlight the various relations existing between music, tourism, heritage and urban geography, and we will investigate how the five chapters in this book contribute to the advancement of these topics in music geography.

Keywords Music geographies • Popular music • Music scenes • Interdisciplinary study of music • Cultural geography • Urban geography • Heritage studies • Music tourism • Placemaking

Over the last few decades, a rich body of literature has explored the importance of music to understand the spatial dimensions of society. These geographic approaches to music are varied, depending on the background of the researchers. While music has generated a substantial interest among geographers, scholars in other disciplines have also developed related spatial perspectives on music. These multiple approaches to the geographies of popular music are the ones that our book series bring together. This volume is the second installment of a three-part book series *New Geographies of Music*. In this introduction, we will explore these perspectives, discuss how they provide a multitude of lenses through which we can study popular music, and how the five chapters in this book contribute to the advancement of music geography.

1 THE GEOGRAPHIES OF MUSIC: UNDERSTANDING THE ROLE OF MUSIC IN THE CONSTRUCTION OF SPACE AND PLACE

During recent decades, music has become a legitimate object of analysis among geographers. While some pioneering works on music and sound go back to the 1920s (Cornish, 1928), the first comprehensive wave of works occurred in the 1970s (e.g., Ford, 1971; Carney, 1978). This early music geography investigated the place of music in local, national, and global contexts; the relationship between soundscapes and specific places;

the diffusion and distribution of musical styles; and geographical imagery in lyrics (see Leyshon et al., 1995).

While the study of music was situated at the margins of the discipline for some time, its position strengthened in the 1990s and 2000s. This evolution was part of broader changes in geography where a "cultural turn" led many researchers toward an interest in cultural, creative, and artistic practices (Aitken & Valentine, 2009). The cultural turn transformed the study of music as a new generation of geographers adopted a variety of new approaches. Several seminal publications published at that time argued that the geography of music is more than highlighting the sites where music is produced (or diffused from) or about places mentioned in songs. It is also about how spatiality—a socially constructed geography—plays a role in the formation and creation of music, and how it reflects "mutually generative relations of music and place" (Leyshon et al., 1995, p. 425).

Building on that momentum, the geography of music has continued to contribute to the discipline at large. In particular, a new interest regarding the role of sound as part of bodily, physical experiences has challenged a discipline often focused on visual dimensions and representations (Bonner-Thompson & Hopkins, 2017). Other works have also illustrated how music can build links between academic geographers and artists and practitioners (see, for example, Hracs et al., 2016 and Zendel, 2023 in *New Geographies of Music 1*). In the book *Sound Tracks*, Connell and Gibson (2003) proposed ways to overcome the global/local dichotomy often used in conceptualizing globalization, arguing that, in music, both spatial manifestations take place at the same time. They suggested instead the concepts of fluidity and fixity as central to understanding the spatiality of musical practices. That is, how music is always mobile and thus subject to change as it moves across space, while also shaped by local forces and becomes fixed in place.

Moreover, geographers became interested in adopting a spatial lens to understand musical practices that until then had mostly been within the purview of other disciplines. In particular, geographical perspectives reexamined all dimensions of music practices, from production and consumption (Hracs et al., 2016) to local music cultures (Kong, 1995) and the global reach of the mainstream music industry (Connell & Gibson, 2003). In doing so, music geographers are not always making a strict distinction between popular music and other musical forms. In various publications, popular music has been studied alongside classical music (Leyshon et al.,

1995), folk music (Revill & Gold, 2018), and within the context of a broader geography of sounds (Anderson et al., 2005; Wissman, 2014).

Reading the work of music geographers, it is evident that all studies cannot be subsumed under one single theoretical umbrella. As Johansson and Bell (2009) explain it, there are "multiple perspectives on the relationships among music and geography; perspectives that are eclectic in terms of research methodology and underlying philosophy" (p. 2). This has sometimes been linked to the nature of musical activity in itself, which "cannot be contained with a single explanatory theory" as music culture is "dynamic and unpredictable, involving movements of sounds and people, expressing mobility in certain period, stability in others" (Connell & Gibson, 2003, p. 17). The result is a sense that music geography research has not led to the emergence of an overarching theory, given that "there are as many musical geographies as there are geographers" (Guiu, 2006). This fragmentation has been accentuated by a lack of awareness from Anglophone researchers regarding the work produced in other languages, despite the rise of significant research in, for example, French (Guiu, 2006; Canova, 2014), Italian (dell'Agnese & Tabusi, 2016; dell'Agnese, 2019), and Portuguese (Panitz, 2012; Dozena, 2016). While researchers in the non-Anglophone world often cite work produced in English, the contrary is rarely true, despite the fact that some of these publications propose innovative theoretical perspectives for the discipline, grounded in their national disciplinary debates (see, for example, a discussion on the idea of "territory" in Canova, 2013).

Therefore, rather than arriving at a common approach, music geographers have pursued various theoretical strains developed within the discipline, following the evolutions of multiple debates. In particular, but without intending to be exhaustive, we want to mention three important (and interrelated) perspectives. In relation to social and cultural geography, the study of music has evolved from an emphasis on lyrics as the carrier of meaning (Leyshon et al., 1995) to a focus on musical practices and performances, in the context of broader calls in the discipline for approaching the world as lived and embodied rather than just represented (Wood et al., 2007; Anderson & Harrison, 2016). More recently, works have also unveiled the material culture of musical objects, for example, through the production of instruments such as guitars (Gibson & Warren, 2021). The study of economic music geography has also made an important contribution. This includes seminal works using music to explore creative economy clustering (Scott, 1999; Florida & Jackson, 2010; Watson, 2008), studies addressing the music industry through the circulation of music production and songs in globalized networks (Johansson, 2020), the impact of digital technology (Leyshon, 2014; Hracs et al., 2016), the nature of work within the confined space of the studio (Watson, 2014), and the entrepreneurial strategies of musicians (Mbaye, 2011). Finally, the perspectives of urban geography have also been crucial. In addition to studies that explore how music conveys geographical imaginaries of urban environments (Guillard, 2016), a wave of public policies aiming to attract and promote creativity has generated scholarly interest in analyzing the impacts of music-led urban (re)development policies (Ballico & Watson, 2020). Here, music geographers have been at the forefront of contextualizing and critiquing the idea of the "creative city" (Florida, 2002), while also providing critical accounts regarding the way music is used to reinforce the city's attractiveness in the context of global inter-urban competition.

2 Understanding the Spatial Dimension of Music Worlds Beyond the Discipline of Geography

Far from limited to geography, research on the spatial dimensions of music has also been carried out in other fields of study. Such approaches have been quite diverse, adopted by researchers in musicology (Krims, 2007; Whiteley et al., 2004), anthropology (Stokes, 1997), sociology (Holt & Wergin, 2013; Bennett, 2000), and media studies (Stahl & Percival, 2022). In many cases, they are linked to a renewed interest in space and place initiated by a geographical turn (Straw quoted in Janotti Jr., 2012) in many disciplines during the 1990s and 2000s. While some of these studies exhibit familiarity with the debates in geography, most of them approached the spatial dimension of musical practices using theoretical models and discussions of their own discipline. This has led to approaches which, while addressing concerns that are close to the perspective of geographers, have often emerged independently, and do not necessarily engage in a dialog with geographic research.

This observation is also true of interdisciplinary fields specifically dedicated to the study of music. The 1980s saw the emergence of popular music studies, and since the 1990s, many researchers in this field have highlighted the importance of the spatial dimension of music. While geographers have mainly been interested in the role of music in the production of space and place, popular music studies address spatiality through songs and music practices. This led to the rise of theoretical models distinct from the ones mobilized by music geographers; in particular, studies focused on music genres as sites of production for geographical imaginaries that evolved through time and at the intersection of race, class, and gender (Peterson, 1997; Forman, 2002). Embedded in these studies was also a discussion around space as a crucial dimension in the construction of "authenticity" within music genres. Other works focused more on the contexts of music activities, mainly through the emergence of "scenes," an idea which has generated important debates about the geographies of artistic worlds, and ways of approaching the concept theoretically and empirically (Straw, 1991; Bennett & Peterson, 2004; Kruse, 2003; Woo et al., 2015; Guibert & Bellavance, 2014). More recently, these issues are also analyzed through the "ecology" of local music (see, for example, Van der Hoeven et al., 2020). Much like the concept of scene, ecology emphasizes the rooting of music actors in a broader environment. The music ecosystem concept, though, bridges the dichotomy of music industry and scenes by incorporating people, entities, and structures often excluded from how both music industry and scenes are usually conceptualized (Behr et al., 2016). Concrete ecology is also addressed in ecomusicology, an interdisciplinary endeavor that emerged in the 2000s, which "considers the relationships of music, culture, and nature; i.e., it is the study of musical and sonic issues, both textual and performative, as they relate to ecology and the environment" (Allen, 2011, p. 392). Despite the centrality of nature-society interaction in geography, ecomusicology has yet to penetrate the discipline, with precious few exceptions (Tyner et al., 2016).

3 THE INCREASING HYBRIDIZATION OF THE STUDY OF SPACE AND MUSIC

We should acknowledge that the analysis of music carried out in geography and in other fields of study have not always been disconnected from each other. Reading the literature in geography, we notice references to spatial approaches developed elsewhere. For example, Leyshon et al. (1995) ground their work in cultural and media studies (from historical figures like Theodor Adorno to contemporary scholars like Will Straw) and Connell and Gibson (2003) cover the debates and approaches developed in popular music studies, such as scenes and authenticity. Similarly, Johansson and Bell (2009) build on work that address geographical features of popular music, but not necessarily originating in geography. Reverse quotations can also be found by researchers in other disciplines. Popular music studies have mobilized the theoretical background developed in geography, from the cultural and social approaches of Edward Soja to the Marxist perspective on the organization and evolution of the American city by David Harvey, or the work on youth cultures by Skelton and Valentine (Forman, 2002; Krims, 2007; Stahl, 2004).

While debates have remained somewhat compartmentalized, trends of cross-fertilization are evident within and outside geography. For example, musicology has embraced social and cultural theory and geographers have moved from a focus on the extra-musical to music in itself, in order to understand "what music and sound do rather that what either represents" (Anderson et al., 2005, p. 640). Thus, a sensible evolution can be noticed, as recent research shows an increased hybridization of approaches that were originally separate. For example, there is interdisciplinary hybridization on issues relating to scenes and urban/tourism policies (Bolderman, 2020), or the emergence of networks such as the urban music scholars' network (see urbanmusicstudies.org) which aims to gather scholars from various backgrounds. This also reflected in that Palgrave Pivot's Geographies of Media books are not just written by geographers, an initiative that aims to foster encounters between geographers and researchers in other disciplines. Therefore, while Johansson and Bell concluded in 2009 that there was no recent edited volume on music geography, now there are an increasing number of books that are dealing with one or several aspects of music/space/place relationships, though they are not always written by geographers (Baker, 2019; Ballico, 2021; Stahl & Percival, 2022).

With increasing production, growing hybridization of research, but also intellectual fragmentation by subtheme, one may wonder if there is still a need for a series of edited books dedicated to music geography. We think that such initiative is important for several reasons:

- It contributes to the coherence of the discussion on music, space, and place, as well as to the dialog between the perspectives developed by geographers and those that have emerged in other disciplines;
- It highlights emerging as well as established avenues of research in music geography, through the work of researchers who are actively engaged in these debates and/or bring new perspectives to them;

8   S. GUILLARD ET AL.

- And it covers theoretical perspectives on the evolving relationship between music, space and place, as well as introducing new empirical case studies.

This book series is the result of an effort during the past few years to generate a dialog among researchers interested in music geography. In particular, it evolved from multiple paper sessions that gathered more than 30 scholars, organized at the American Association of Geographers (AAG) annual meetings. While paying attention to the legacy of music, space, and place, this book series also expands into new directions. To this end, the *New Geographies of Music* reflect contemporary music research, whether shedding light on increasingly significant aspects of this topic or developing new theoretical and methodological perspectives.

While previous edited collections on music geography adopted the format of a single book or a journal issue aiming to encompass multiple dimensions, we have decided to publish three Palgrave Pivot monographs oriented around separate but related perspectives. While recognizing that the growth of research on the geographies of music may lead to atomization around specific subthemes, it is also important to maintain a common conversation. Therefore, we decided to design our series as three books where each explores a bundle of interrelated themes so the reader has the option focus on one set of issues or, more expansively (which is preferable), read all three.

Obviously, *New Geographies of Music* does not intend to cover the full spectrum of research in music geography, as it is dependent on the topics and case studies chosen by individual chapter authors. Yet, we hope that it can provide a way for researchers to navigate a multitude of discourses at the intersection of music and geography, as well as to provide a basis for further development of the field.

4   New Geographies of Music 2: Music in Urban Tourism, Heritage Politics, and Place-Making

4.1   Main Issues

The background to this second installment of the *New Geographies of Music* series is the increasing role that music has acquired in urban tourism over the past decades, and its consequences on heritage and place-making strategies. While cities have long been prime sites for the development of music scenes and industries (see *New Geographies of Music 1*), a number of them have become in recent times the focus of tourism and heritage practices and policies. While these issues are now being addressed more broadly by a growing literature,[1] our volume specifically aims to address the role of tourism and heritage within the context of urban geographies of music. Based on the literature, it seems that the relation between music, tourism and heritage, and urban geography can be approached in (at least) three different ways: through the representation of urban touristic destinations within songs, by examining the role of music within the touristic experience associated with urban spaces, and by observing how music can trigger new touristic and heritage practices.

First, music has long been known for conveying imaginaries on a variety of geographical places (see *New Geographies of Music 3*). Depending on the type of material (songs, videos, album covers), artists, or genres, these imaginaries have been associated with experiences of both "here and now" and of the past from the vantage point of elsewhere. As shown in Chap. 3 of this volume, the representation of Buenos Aires in famous tango songs is not just one of an intimate, lived-in city, practiced on a daily basis, but also as an object of nostalgia, conveyed by faraway musicians missing a city that is now long gone. Music has also been a prime medium to understand movements between places. This dimension is particularly clear in pop music from the sixties and the seventies, where traveling is central to the lyrical and visual content developed by many artists (Powell, 1988; Gibson & Connell, 2005). Therefore, it is not surprising that the analysis of songs can help to understand touristic experiences. For example, in a book where he scrutinizes a corpus of French pop songs, Olivier Lazzarotti (2021) highlights how they appear as a great "pedagogical tool" to uncover mainstream representations of vacations, and the way they are approached and lived by a variety of individuals.[2]

In addition to being a medium to understand tourism and heritage processes, music can also be a part of touristic experiences of cities. As noticed by Connell and Gibson (2003), few holiday brochures are

---

[1] See, for example, the literature reviews provided by Gibson and Connell (2005), Lashua et al. (2014), Bolderman (2020, 2022), and Watson (2018) for music tourism, and Cohen et al. (2014) and Strong (2022) for music heritage.

[2] A similar tone, see the issue on "Tourism and Musical Imaginaries," published in *Via Tourism Review* (Gravari-Barbas et al., 2023).

without references to music, whether they appear through bars, clubs, shows, or folklore. Indeed, music is frequently involved in different stages of the touristic experience, whether it is about imagining future destinations through the lens of music or listening to songs associated with the visited place when the tourists return home (Bolderman, 2022). Over the past decades, this dimension has been reinforced by the fact that in a postindustrial context, culture, arts, and events have become central tools in the growing competition among cities across the world (Zukin, 1995). Following the creative city model in the early 2000s, many cities started to conduct culture-led regeneration strategies based on the idea of appearing as vibrant, festive, and eventful places (Richards & Palmer, 2010). Music plays a role in these evolutions; concerts and festivals are elements that can contribute to create an atmosphere, enhance the experience of a city, and even sometimes become a "pull" factor for tourists who starts to "travel to hear music played" (Lashua et al., 2014, p. 8). Therefore, while some urban authorities have worked on developing music festivals which can add to their existing touristic offerings, the image of specific places, from Ibiza to Austin, are intrinsically linked to the idea of having dynamic live scenes that can be experienced by residents and tourists alike (Wynn, 2015; Sandvoss, 2014).

Finally, in a number of urban destinations, the live music dimension has been reinforced by the presence of a strong local music history that makes them particularly relevant places to visit for music fans. Over the past century, the rise of transnational industry networks for the diffusion of music has turned songs into powerful mediums through which the images of specific local—and especially urban—places are experienced globally. This leads numerous fans to develop a powerful and intimate relation with cities that they might have never visited, in a process that Leonieke Bolderman calls "musical topophilia" (2020). Bolderman identifies four main ways through which fans connect music with specific places: specific localized "sounds"; geographical imaginaries of non-musical aspects of music (like lyrics or album covers); locations linked to the biography of the artists; and associations with places where music is (or was once) produced, distributed, or consumed (Bolderman, 2020). By draping places with new values of authenticity and nostalgia, this musical topophilia has been at the source of a growing form of niche tourism, in which music triggers new tourism practices (Gibson & Connell, 2005).

Previous research on music tourism has highlighted the existence of many urban hot spots for music tourism: these can be linked to specific artists or groups, such as Liverpool and the Beatles (Cohen, 2007) or Graceland and Elvis (Alderman, 2009), high-profile events like in Austin (O'Meara & Tretter, 2013), or place-based music genres like Harlem and jazz (Guedj, 2010). On this level, scholars have highlighted how, far from just accompanying the practices of touristic destinations, music can become a new lens, a "musicalized tourist gaze" (Bennett, 2002), through which geographical places are as perceived and practiced. For example, in a study about blues tourism in Chicago, Grazian highlighted how the tourists' approach to the city is heavily influenced by their idea of the genre. From the "commodified" downtown to the African-American neighborhoods on the South and West side, their tastes in blues lead them to favor different parts of the city, in order to visit clubs that they perceive as more "authentic" (Grazian, 2004).

Given their potential for generating commerce or enhancing local identities, these touristic practices have raised the interest of many stakeholders who have started to develop policies specifically dedicated to promote cities as (past or present) sites of music-making. Those stakeholders include a diverse group of actors, ranging from local music fans to large non-profit institutions, corporations or city governments. For this reason, it is not surprising that music tourism development strategies have been taking many shapes, from heritage tours dedicated to specific artists (the Beatles) or genres (hip-hop) (Feifan Xie et al., 2007), to recurring festivals (New Orleans Jazz and Heritage Festival), processes of labeling for a style of music (e.g., tango and flamenco), or the creation of museums celebrating a local scene (see the literature review by Christina Ballico in this volume). While these initiatives often emerged independently, recent years have seen the rise of more coordinated city-wide strategies, especially through the use of a new "music city" framework (Ballico & Watson, 2020; Johansson, 2023 in *New Geographies of Music 1*).

The development of initiatives, policies, and infrastructures dedicated to music tourism has had many impacts on the cities where they have emerged. On an artistic level, they have led to efforts to preserve the memory of local scenes and have them promoted as part of the local heritage, and such efforts have been increasing as artists, genres, and fans are aging (Cohen et al., 2014). While the promotion of music tourism has helped this process, research also shows how the recognition of one local music scene could also create new divides locally. The Liverpool case is an emblematic one: while tourism focused on the Beatles has been a central asset in countering the industrial decline experienced by the city (Connell

12   S. GUILLARD ET AL.

& Gibson, 2003), it has also led to the marginalization of other genres, like country, in the narratives about the history of the local scene (Cohen, 2007).

On a spatial and urban level, the transformation of former sites of creativity, production, and performance into tourist sites has also led to major social changes in some neighborhoods. While music tourism has had positive impacts in terms of image or economic revenue for some cities, it has also been criticized for reinforcing social and racial inequalities within touristic destinations, and creating gentrified touristic enclaves within marginalized areas. When studying the case of Memphis, Gibson and Connell (2007) notice, for example, that Graceland, which now serves as a museum dedicated to Elvis Presley, is visited mainly by white tourists, despite being located in the middle of a predominantly black neighborhood. Similarly, music tourism in Memphis has been central to the regeneration of Beale Street (Johansson, 2010), which had once been central to the development of blues and rock'n'roll, before becoming derelict in the 1960s. Its renewal as a touristic attraction dedicated to the history of music in Memphis has had a strong impact on the surrounding housing market, leading to the displacement of many former (predominantly black) local residents. On this level, concerns about the role of music tourism on place-making meet broader criticism about tourism policies as a whole. Nevertheless, the fact remains that "where urban landscapes are reconstructed for tourist consumption, marginalization of certain social groups is commonplace" (Gibson & Connell, 2007, pp. 184–185).

4.2   Outline of the Chapters

Bringing together researchers from various disciplinary and geographical backgrounds, the chapters of this book complement the reflections above by exploring various dimensions and evolutions of the intertwined relations among music and tourism, heritage, and place-making.

Following this introduction, the first two chapters highlight how, in a globalized context, the diffusion of translocal music movements and singular artistic projects are influencing the production of touristified urban areas. Chapter 2, "Music in Surf Town Typology: Alternative Spaces of a Subculture," analyses, through the example of surf music, how music practices can have a significant role in shaping the "feel" of a touristic town, and influence the way urban space is practiced and conceived. Anne Barjolin-Smith explores the case of an iconic surf town, Cocoa Beach in

Florida, where surfing has long defined the area. In this context, music is an element that contributes to the town's singular character, as it enables the global movement of surfing and surf music to take root in the town's public spaces. Music also appears as a way for various individuals to signify an appropriation of space in the context of a town marked by debates on authenticity. Therefore, while the "soundscape" of the Cocoa Beach is an important element in touristic experiences, music performances are also a way for surfers to "reclaim their space" as one of an "authentic" lifestyle, although this idea of authenticity is partly commodified by "lifestyle brands."

The role of music in defining the atmosphere of public spaces, in the context of increasingly connected cities, is also central in Chap. 3, "Street Piano: An Instrument of Urban Change." In this chapter, Alenka Barber-Kersovan explores the case of the free-to-use street pianos that have proliferated in various cities in the world. Originally designed as an art project from the British artist Luke Jerram, the pianos were conceived as a way for passers-by to "claim ownership of their urban landscape" through music-ing, with the goal of reinforcing local senses of place, and enhancing ties among urban communities. In this regard, the Street Piano project echoes a growing trend of "eventification" of cities, which aim to generate new emotions in relation to the practice of urban spaces. Yet, the Street Piano project also intersects with the desire of various urban authorities and private actors to make urban spaces appear as more "vibrant" in order to attract a variety of residents and visitors. By tracing the diffusion and the evolution of the Street Piano initiative, the chapter explores the tensions between the original artistic initiative, which was promoted as a way to "bring positive change within the city," and its increasing use in the context of a "festivalization" of public spaces, which serves the interests of urban growth coalitions. While this chapter follows the literature that has highlighted how music is an integral part of the marketing strategies of cities across the world, it also furthers a perspective that has often been limited to studying the valorization of local scenes as assets, especially in the context of the "Music Cities" paradigm (Ballico & Watson, 2020; Johansson, 2023 in *New Geographies of Music 1*).

While the first two chapters observe how global movements and artistic initiatives could contribute to local place-making and tourism strategies in urban spaces, the three other chapters of this edited book are addressing the reverse process: how, and to what extent, localized music scenes can become the object of heritage and tourism policies, and what consequences it has both on musical practices and the spaces where they have originally emerged. Chapter 4, "Tango music: Between Heritage and Transnational Resources. The Geographies of Tango in or from Buenos Aires," analyzes these issues by tracing the global diffusion and transformation of a single genre, thanks to multi-sited investigations carried out in Buenos Aires, Montevideo, and Paris. Developed originally in Argentina (and to a lesser extent in Uruguay), tango went through a heritage process over the past decades, with a significant milestone being its inclusion on UNESCO's Representative List of the Intangible Cultural Heritage of Humanity. Elsa Broclain, Francesca Cominelli, Sébastien Jacquot, and Elodie Salin argue that these heritage policies have led to new divides within tango's practices. While the practice of tango is strongly linked to the *music* practiced in the milonga events of Buenos Aires and Montevideo, a type of practice that is still at the center of contemporary iterations in specialized venues globally, heritage policies have been driven first and foremost by a preservation of the *dance* repertoire associated with a former "golden age." This situation impacts the trajectories and career paths of musicians. From Buenos Aires to Paris, they learn to navigate between heritage-oriented scenes, marked by the pre-eminence of dance, and more intimate ones focused on music, each of them associated with contradictory expectations and norms. By exploring the influence of heritage and tourism policies from the perspective of the global practices of artists, this chapter provides a good counterpoint to studies that had focused on the touristification of local music scenes through the sole perspective of touristic practices (Grazian, 2004).

While heritage and tourism policies have an influence on the global practices of musicians, it also impacts the presence of music in local urban spaces. In Chap. 5, "Taking Music to the (Museum) Masses: Museum Engagement with the Country and Grunge Music Heritages of Nashville and Seattle," Christina Ballico explores these issues by comparing the role that two major popular music museums have acquired in two US cities: the Country Music Hall of Fame in Nashville and Museum of Popular Culture in Seattle. These museums are good points of comparison as they both illustrate the recognition of a local music scene within one specific music genre (country and grunge respectively). While these institutions signify the inclusion of local musical heritage within the touristic experience of both cities, they also provide a specific take on the music genres and their rooting in local urban spaces, as their location and curatorial practices contribute to the selection of specific narratives, actors, and places to the detriment of others. In her analysis, Christina Ballico compares the rooting of the museums within their respective locales by observing their inclusion in the official tourism campaign of the city, the structure of their permanent and temporary exhibitions, and their geographical position within their downtown district. This chapter contributes to a growing literature on the showcasing of popular music within museum settings (Baker et al., 2019), while initiating a comparative approach on the role that these institutions have in showcasing and preserving the narratives and activities associated with genre and place-based music scenes.

The heritage of music scenes with a rich history is not always promoted as much as it is in Nashville and Seattle. What makes a city a center for music tourism and what prevents it from being so? In the final chapter, Leonieke Bolderman analyzes this issue through the case of Detroit. In her chapter, "The Hidden Music City: the Role of Music Tourism Imaginaries in the Regeneration of Detroit," she observes that, even though Detroit has a rich music history and a vibrant music scene, this dimension has often remained a marginal element in the development strategy conducted by the local authorities. This is all the more surprising as music could play a vital role in the effort to regenerate a city that has been marked by a long-term economic and demographic decline. According to Bolderman, the reason comes from the fact that music is a source of both divisions and belonging for local communities. Therefore, while the use of music has the potential of recreating positive images that counteract the idea of a struggling city, the transformation of venues and events into touristic and heritage landmarks can also easily revive racial and social tensions regarding the use of local urban spaces. The city-wide policies and case studies analyzed in this chapter helps to nuance the strategies of music tourism development as promoted within the context of the "music cities" framework. It shows that the development of a music tourism and heritage strategy is not just about developing policy instruments, but also about taking in account the imaginaries and mythologies that have long shaped local music scenes, and thinking about whose stories are being told and whose remain hidden.

References

Aitken, S., & Valentine, G. (2009). *Approaches to human geography*. Sage.
Alderman, D. (2009). Writing on the Graceland wall: On the importance of authorship in pilgrimage landscapes. In O. Johansson & T. L. Bell (Eds.), *Sound, society, and the geography of popular music*. Ashgate.

Allen, A. (2011). Ecomusicology: Ecocriticism and musicology. *Journal of the American Musicological Society, 64*(2), 391–394.

Anderson, B., & Harrison, P. (2016). *Taking-place: Non-representational theories and geography.* Routledge.

Anderson, B., Morton, F., & Revill, G. (Eds.). (2005). Practice of music and sound. *Social & Cultural Geography, 6*(5), 639–644.

Baker, A. J. (2019). *The great music city: Exploring music, space and identity.* Palgrave Macmillan.

Baker, S., Istvandity, L., & Nowak, R. (2019). *Curating pop: Exhibiting Popular music in the museum.* Bloomsbury Academic.

Ballico, C. (Ed.). (2021). *Geographically isolated and peripheral music scenes: Global insights and perspectives.* Palgrave Macmillan.

Ballico, C., & Watson, A. (Eds.). (2020). *Music cities. Evaluating a global cultural policy concept.* Palgrave Macmillan.

Behr, A., Brennan, M., Cloonan, M., Frith, S., & Webster, E. (2016). Live concert performance – An ecological approach. *Rock Music Studies, 3*, 5–23.

Bennett, A. (2000). *Popular music and youth culture: Music identity and place.* Macmillan.

Bennett, A. (2002). Music, media and urban mythscapes: A study of the "Canterbury Sound". *Media, Culture and Society, 24*, 87–100.

Bennett, A., & Peterson, R. (2004). *Music scenes: Local, translocal and virtual.* Vanderbilt University Press.

Bolderman, L. (2020). *Contemporary music tourism: A theory of musical topophilia.* Routledge.

Bolderman, L. (2022). Music and tourism. In G. Stahl & M. Percival (Eds.), *The Bloomsbury handbook of popular music and place* (pp. 341–356). Bloomsbury.

Bonner-Thompson, C., & Hopkins, P. (2017). *Geographies of the body.* Oxford University Press.

Canova, N. (2013). Music in French geography as space marker and placer maker. *Social & Cultural Geography, 14*(8), 861–867.

Canova, N. (2014). *La Musique au coeur de l'analyse géographique.* L'Harmattan.

Carney, G. (Ed.). (1978). *The sounds of people and places.* University Press of America.

Cohen, S. (2007). *Decline, renewal and the city in popular music culture: Beyond the Beatles.* Ashgate.

Cohen, S., Roberts, L., Knifton, R., & Leonard, M. (2014). *Sites of popular music heritage. Memories, histories, places.* Routledge.

Connell, J., & Gibson, C. (2003). *Sound tracks, popular music, identity and place.* Routledge.

Cornish, V. (1928). Harmonies of scenery: An outline of aesthetic geography. *Geography, 14*, 275–282, 383–339.

dell'Agnese, E. (2019). Musica (popolare) e spazi urbani: una introduzione. *Rivista Geografica Italiana.* https://www.francoangeli.it/riviste/Scheda_rivista.aspx?IDArticolo=65196

dell'Agnese, E., & Tabusi, M. (Eds.). (2016). *La musica come geografia: suoni, luoghi, territori.* Società Geografica Italiana. http://societageografica.net/wp/wp-content/uploads/2016/09/La_musica_come_geografia_ebook.pdf

Dozena, A. (Ed.). (2016). *Geografia e Música. Diálogos.* Edufrn.

Feifan Xie, P., Osumare, H., & Ibrahim, A. (2007). Gazing the hood: Hip-hop as tourism attraction. *Tourism Management, 28,* 452–460.

Florida, R. (2002). *The rise of the creative class: And how it's transforming work, leisure, community and everyday life.* Basic Books.

Florida, R., & Jackson, S. (2010). Sonic city: The evolving economic geography of the music industry. *Journal of Planning Education and Research, 29*(3), 310–321.

Ford, L. (1971). Geographic factors in the origin, evolution, and diffusion of rock and roll music. *Journal of Geography, 70*(8), 455–464.

Forman, M. (2002). *The hood comes first: Race, space and place in rap and hip-hop.* Wesleyan.

Gibson, C., & Connell, J. (2005). *Music and tourism: On the road again.* Channel View Publications.

Gibson, C., & Connell, J. (2007). Music, tourism and the transformation of Memphis. *Tourism Geographies, 9*(2), 160–190.

Gibson, C., & Warren, A. (2021). *The guitar. Tracing the grain back to the tree.* University of Chicago Press.

Gravari-Barbas, M., Graburn, N., & Staszak, J.-F. (2023). Tourism and musical imaginaries. *Via Tourism Review, 23.* https://doi.org/10.4000/viatourism.9998

Grazian, D. (2004). The symbolic economy of authenticity in the Chicago blues scene. In A. Bennett & R. Peterson (Eds.), *Music scenes. Local, translocal and virtual* (pp. 31–47). Vanderbilt University Press.

Guedj, P. (2010). Jazz et tourisme. Construction et Patrimonialisation d'une musique noire aux Etats-Unis. *Géographie et Cultures, 76,* 31–46.

Guibert, G., & Bellavance, G. (Eds.). (2014). La notion de "scène", entre sociologie de la culture et sociologie urbaine: génèse, actualité et perspectives. *Cahiers de la recherche sociologique, 57,* 5–180.

Guillard, S. (2016). *Musique, ville et scènes. Localisation et production de l'authenticité dans le rap en France et aux Etats-Unis.* Doctoral thesis, Université Paris Est.

Guiu, C. (2006). *Géographie et Musique, quelles perspectives?* Géographie et Cultures, n°59. L'Harmattan.

Holt, F., & Wergin, C. (2013). *Musical performance and the changing city. Postindustrial contexts in Europe and the United States.* Routledge.

Hracs, B., Seman, M., & Virani, T. (2016). *The production and consumption of music in the digital age*. Routledge.

Janotti, J., Jr. (2012). Interview – Will Straw and the importance of music scenes in music and communication studies. *Revista de Associação National dos Programas de Pos-Graduação, 15*(2).

Johansson, O. (2010). Form, function, and the development of music-themed entertainment districts in Nashville and Memphis. *Material Culture, 42*(1), 47–69.

Johansson, O. (2020). *Songs from Sweden. Shaping pop culture in a globalized music industry*. Palgrave Macmillan.

Johansson, O. (2023). The music cities movement and circulation of best practices. In O. Johansson, S. Guillard, & J. Palis (Eds.), *New Geographies of Music 1: Urban policies, live music, and careers in a changing industry* (pp. 39–65). Palgrave Macmillan.

Johansson, O., & Bell, T. (2009). *Sound, society and the geography of popular music*. Ashgate.

Kong, L. (1995). Popular music and a "sense of place" in Singapore. *Crossroads, 9*(2), 51–77.

Krims, A. (2007). *Music and urban geography*. Routledge.

Kruse, H. (2003). *Site and sound: Understanding independent music scenes*. Peter Lang.

Lashua, B., Spracklen, K., & Long, R. (2014). Introduction to the special issue: Music and tourism. *Tourist Studies, 14*(1), 3–9.

Lazzarotti, O. (2021). *Vivent les vacances ! Tourisme et chansons*. Presses Universitaires du Septentrion.

Leyshon, A. (2014). *Reformatted: Code, networks, and the transformation of the music industry*. Oxford University Press.

Leyshon, A., Matless, D., & Revill, G. (1995). The place of music [Introduction]. *Transactions of the Institute of British Geographers, 20*(4), 423–433.

Mbaye, J. (2011). *Reconsidering cultural entrepreneurship: Hip hop music economy and social change in Senegal, francophone West Africa*. Doctoral thesis, The London School of Economics and Political Science (LSE).

O'Meara, C., & Tretter, E. (2013). Sounding Austin: Live music, race, and the selling of a city. In F. Holt & C. Wergin (Eds.), *Musical performance and the changing city* (pp. 52–76). Routledge.

Panitz, L. (2012). Geografia e música: uma introdução ao tema. *Biblio3W. Revista bibliográfica de geografia y ciencias sociales, XVII*(978) http://www.ub.edu/geocrit/b3w-978.htm

Peterson, R. (1997). *Creating country music, Fabricating authenticity*. University of Chicago Press.

Powell, A. (1988). Like a rolling stone: Notions of youth travel and tourism in pop music of the sixties, seventies, and eighties, *Kroeber anthropological society papers*, 67–68, 28–34.

Revill, G., & Gold, J. R. (2018). "Far back in American time": Culture, region, nation, Appalachia, and the geography of voice. *Annals of the American Association of Geographers, 108*(5), 1406–1421.

Richards, G., & Palmer, R. (2010). *Eventful cities: Cultural management and urban revitalisation.* Elsevier.

Sandvoss, C. (2014). I (heart) Ibiza. Music, place and belonging. In M. Duffet (Ed.), *Popular music fandom: Identities, roles and practices* (pp. 115–145). Routledge.

Scott, A. J. (1999). The US recorded music industry: On the relations between organization, location, and creativity in the cultural economy. *Environment and Planning A, 31*, 1965–1984.

Stahl, G. (2004). It's like Canada reduced. Setting the scene in Montreal. In A. Bennett & K. Kahn-Harris (Eds.), *After subculture* (pp. 51–56). Palgrave Macmillan.

Stahl, G., & Percival, M. (2022). *The Bloomsbury handbook of popular music, space and place.* Bloomsbury.

Stokes, M. (1997). *Ethnicity, identity and music: The musical construction of place.* Berg.

Straw, W. (1991). System of articulation and logic of change: Communities and scenes in popular music. *Cultural Studies, 5*(3), 368–388.

Strong, C. (2022). Music, heritage and place. In G. Stahl & M. Percival (Eds.), *The Bloomsbury handbook of popular music and place* (pp. 331–339). Bloomsbury.

Tyner, J., Rhodes, M., & Kimsroy, S. (2016). Music, nature, power, and place: An Ecomusicology of Khmer Rouge songs. *GeoHumanities, 2*(2), 395–412.

Van der Hoeven, A., Hitters, E., Berkers, P., Mulder, M., & Everts, R. (2020). Theorizing the production and consumption of live music. A critical review. In E. Marzierska, L. Gillon, & T. Rigg (Eds.), *The future of music* (pp. 19–33). Bloomsbury Publishing.

Watson, A. (2008). Global music city: Knowledge and geographical proximity in London's recorded music industry. *Area, 40*(1), 12–23.

Watson, A. (2014). *Cultural production in and beyond the recording studio.* Routledge.

Watson, A. (2018). Music tourism. In S. Agarwal, G. Busby, & R. Huang (Eds.), *Special interest tourism: Concepts, contexts and cases* (pp. 73–84). CAB International.

Whiteley, S., Bennett, A., & Hawkins, S. (2004). *Music, space and place: Popular music and cultural identity.* Routledge.

Wissman, T. (2014). *Geographies of urban sound*. Ashgate.

Woo, B., Rennie, J., & Poyntz, S. (Eds.). (2015). Scene thinking. *Cultural Studies, 29*(3), 285–297.

Wood, N., Duffy, M., & Smith, S. (2007). The art of doing (geographies of) music. *Environment and Planning D: Society and Space, 25*(5), 867–889.

Wynn, J. (2015). *Music/city. American festivals and placemaking in Austin, Nashville and Newport*. University of Chicago Press.

Zukin, S. (1995). *The cultures of cities*. Blackwell-Wiley.

CHAPTER 2

Music in Surf Town Typology: Alternative Spaces of a Subculture

Anne Barjolin-Smith

Abstract This piece looks at a Floridian touristic surf town named Cocoa Beach to investigate the role of music in urban space appropriation. This relatively new town, established in 1925, has built its socio-cultural heritage and thriving tourism industry on a singular surf lifestyle anchored in the United State's Southern culture and the Caribbean. The town has enabled the conveyance of the surf lifestyle by allowing representational and inclusive aesthetic dynamics to strive through local enterprise. Among the many instances that illustrate this point, we look at how a Cocoa Beach-based sunscreen company named Sun Bum has dedicated its space to musical performances to promote a local surf lifestyle associated with the surf town. While acknowledging the historical heritage of Californian surf music, Cocoa Beach surfers have developed a musical scene that reflects their laid-back approach to surfing and allows them to define their local community in a global surf culture collectively. As a result, imported and local musics are integrated into the feel of the town and are used as a platform that contributes to marking local identities and economies by promoting a singular "surfanization."

A. Barjolin-Smith (✉)
Florida Virtual School, Orlando, FL, USA

© The Author(s), under exclusive license to Springer Nature Singapore Pte Ltd. 2024
S. Guillard et al. (eds.), *New Geographies of Music 2*, Geographies of Media, https://doi.org/10.1007/978-981-97-2072-9_2

21

Sun Bum's office space usage as a stage is a way to relocalize surf music: it is displaced, branded, and displayed as a Cocoa Beach surf lifestyle and identity. Local surfers see it as validating their singular identity while tourists associate these musical events with the surf town. Infrastructures developed by aesthetic, social, and geographic communities have enabled the growth of a subculture inherited, commodified, and reorganized according to local codes. The process allows the activation of know-hows and clarifies the space-music-activity relationship and the interconnectedness of the global and the local.

Keywords Surfanization • Surf town • Surf music • Soundscape • Surf lifestyle

1 INTRODUCTION

From the physical space in which music comes to life to a mythology built around ideological scenes, the place where a type of music develops plays a vital role in its evolution and conservation. In the most representative or stereotyped places, there is an effort to cultivate, support, and maintain musical activity to locally activate new forms of creative cultures and identities so that these loci are also shaped by the music they nurture. This chapter illustrates this point by showing how surf music, from its origins to its global expansion within localized scenes, has empowered surfers to claim ownership of urban spaces. Specifically, it develops the idea that various types of surf music exist worldwide anchored in geographical and social spaces allowing surfing communities to take possession of their local beaches by conveying their vision of the surf lifestyle. Focusing on a Floridian surf town called Cocoa Beach, I examine how a local sunscreen company named Sun Bum leveraged its surfer-employees to host musical performances at their office to promote a local surf lifestyle at once associated with and shaping the surf town. I emancipate surf music from the myth of an authentic surf culture exclusively marked by 1960s Californian aesthetics. To do so, I explore surf music's implementation and social function in the Floridian surf town, highlighting its impact on the urban environment. Surf music is used as a platform that contributes to marking local identities and local economies, promoting what I call *surfanization,* a singular form of urbanization inspired by surfing. Sun Bum's office space usage as a stage is a way to relocalize surf music: it is displaced, branded, and displayed as Cocoa Beach surf lifestyle and identity. Local surfers perceive this surf music as validating their unique identity while tourists associate these musical events with the surf town.

The research methodology, underpinned by cultural studies concepts, ethnomusicology, and urban geography, consists of a participant observation performed between 2015 and 2019. I engaged in a series of cultural events organized by the town's surf-oriented businesses, including concerts hosted by Sun Bum. I conducted semi-formal interviews of local surfers involved with the surf and or the music industries, like Sun Bum's manager in Cocoa Beach and D.J.s working in collaboration with Sun Bum. The interviews focused on surfers' relationship to music and their sense of belonging to the Floridian surfers' community. In previous research (Barjolin-Smith, 2018a, 2020), I touched upon the status of the surf town as a space for surfers' musicking.[1] This chapter constitutes a more in-depth exploration of both the phenomenology of the surf town's musical sounds and their socio-cultural function. The emphasis is placed on the role of music and locally entertained lifestyles in understanding urban development and experience. Looking at the surf town's soundscape, a concept coined by Raymond Murray Schafer (1977) to define the sonic equivalent of a landscape, I observed and analyzed participants' perceptual responses to their acoustic, aesthetic, and geographic surroundings.

This chapter first describes what constitutes a surf town and what qualifies Cocoa Beach as one. It defines the concept of surf lifestyle and proposes a new interpretation of surf music not as a genre but as a movement composed of localized iterations. Second, the chapter identifies the sonic elements that come into play in the town's organization and analyzes how these sounds shape the urban space by looking at a specific musical event called Sonny's Porch, organized by Sun Bum. Roland Robertson's (1995) notion of glocalization helps explain how a specific construction of surf music gives the town its singular character. Third, the notion of

---

[1] Christopher Small (1998) coined the notion of musicking, which is the gerund of the verb "to music." It covers any activity linked to music. The author defined to music as "to take part, in any capacity, in musical performance, whether by performing, by listening, by rehearsing, or by practicing, by providing material for performance (what is called composing), or by dancing" (p. 9).

24   A. BARJOLIN-SMITH

surfanization is used to illustrate how music's corporeality enables space appropriation by surfers and provides the town with its aesthetic identity.

2   THE SURF TOWN: COCOA BEACH AND THE SURF LIFESTYLE

A surf town is a coastal urban area where the beach and the surf lifestyle and their symbols intertwine. As Vincent Coëffé (2010, 2014) has highlighted, the beach is at once a scenery, a place of leisure and tourism, and a social space. It enables practices that would be deemed inappropriate in other urban contexts, such as being denuded, wearing laid-back attires, or listening to private music in public spaces. The stereotypical surf town is in proximity to warm or tropical waters, and its architecture suggests a beach lifestyle characterized by nautical colors, boating decorations, sea-life representations, surfboard ornaments, etc. These towns developed alongside the advent of paid vacation, beach tourism, and surfing and resulted from Florida's development as a twentieth-century construction (Coëffé, 2010, p. 61). For Chris Gibson and John Connell (2005), the democratization of paid vacation produced a form of tourism "characterized by large numbers of people traveling to seemingly mass-produced resorts in a small number of destinations (characterized, to many, by the rise of tourism in the Costa del Sol, Spain, or in Florida)" (p. 7). Cocoa Beach, a surf town located on the Space Coast of Florida, results from this process. While the town was already promoted in the 1920s as being "one of the pleasure resorts of the States" for its "surf bathing comfortable" waters (Parrish et al., 2001, p. 111), it became the historical hub of surfing on the east coast of the United States in the 1960s.

Surfing is a lifestyle sport, a notion broadly defining sports activities that have emerged from Hawaiian surfing after it was imported and developed in the United States in the 1950s and 1960s.[2] Lifestyle sports are characterized by participants' identification with symbols and ideologies beyond the activity's punctual practice (Wheaton, 2004). These sports include surfing, snowboarding, and skateboarding. As Sylvain Lefebvre and Romain Roult (2009) have shown, these practices have gone from being counter-cultural movements to popular movements that have

---

[2] Hawaiian surfers were seen on the Californian coast as early as the 1880s (Walker, 2011, p. 30), but the practice only took off in the 1950s when the Golden State became "the epicenter of surf media, board manufacturing and design" (Lemarié & Domann, 2019, p. 2).

usage as a stage is a way to relocalize surf music: it is displaced, branded, and displayed as Cocoa Beach surf lifestyle and identity. Local surfers perceive this surf music as validating their unique identity while tourists associate these musical events with the surf town.

The research methodology, underpinned by cultural studies concepts, ethnomusicology, and urban geography, consists of a participant observation performed between 2015 and 2019. I engaged in a series of cultural events organized by the town's surf-oriented businesses, including concerts hosted by Sun Bum. I conducted semi-formal interviews of local surfers involved with the surf and or the music industries, like Sun Bum's manager in Cocoa Beach and D.J.s working in collaboration with Sun Bum. The interviews focused on surfers' relationship to music and their sense of belonging to the Floridian surfers' community. In previous research (Barjolin-Smith, 2018a, 2020), I touched upon the status of the surf town as a space for surfers' musicking.[1] This chapter constitutes a more in-depth exploration of both the phenomenology of the surf town's musical sounds and their socio-cultural function. The emphasis is placed on the role of music and locally entertained lifestyles in understanding urban development and experience. Looking at the surf town's soundscape, a concept coined by Raymond Murray Schafer (1977) to define the sonic equivalent of a landscape, I observed and analyzed participants' perceptual responses to their acoustic, aesthetic, and geographic surroundings.

This chapter first describes what constitutes a surf town and what qualifies Cocoa Beach as one. It defines the concept of surf lifestyle and proposes a new interpretation of surf music not as a genre but as a movement composed of localized iterations. Second, the chapter identifies the sonic elements that come into play in the town's organization and analyzes how these sounds shape the urban space by looking at a specific musical event called Sonny's Porch, organized by Sun Bum. Roland Robertson's (1995) notion of glocalization helps explain how a specific construction of surf music gives the town its singular character. Third, the notion of

---

[1] Christopher Small (1998) coined the notion of musicking, which is the gerund of the verb "to music." It covers any activity linked to music. The author defined to music as "to take part, in any capacity, in musical performance, whether by performing, by listening, by rehearsing, or by practicing, by providing material for performance (what is called composing), or by dancing" (p. 9).

24 A. BARJOLIN-SMITH

surfanization is used to illustrate how music's corporeality enables space appropriation by surfers and provides the town with its aesthetic identity.

2 THE SURF TOWN: COCOA BEACH AND THE SURF LIFESTYLE

A surf town is a coastal urban area where the beach and the surf lifestyle and their symbols intertwine. As Vincent Coëffé (2010, 2014) has highlighted, the beach is at once a scenery, a place of leisure and tourism, and a social space. It enables practices that would be deemed inappropriate in other urban contexts, such as being denuded, wearing laid-back attires, or listening to private music in public spaces. The stereotypical surf town is in proximity to warm or tropical waters, and its architecture suggests a beach lifestyle characterized by nautical colors, boating decorations, sea-life representations, surfboard ornaments, etc. These towns developed alongside the advent of paid vacation, beach tourism, and surfing and resulted from Florida's development as a twentieth-century construction (Coëffé, 2010, p. 61). For Chris Gibson and John Connell (2005), the democratization of paid vacation produced a form of tourism "characterized by large numbers of people traveling to seemingly mass-produced resorts in a small number of destinations (characterized, to many, by the rise of tourism in the Costa del Sol, Spain, or in Florida)" (p. 7). Cocoa Beach, a surf town located on the Space Coast of Florida, results from this process. While the town was already promoted in the 1920s as being "one of the pleasure resorts of the States" for its "surf bathing comfortable" waters (Parrish et al., 2001, p. 111), it became the historical hub of surfing on the east coast of the United States in the 1960s.

Surfing is a lifestyle sport, a notion broadly defining sports activities that have emerged from Hawaiian surfing after it was imported and developed in the United States in the 1950s and 1960s.[2] Lifestyle sports are characterized by participants' identification with symbols and ideologies beyond the activity's punctual practice (Wheaton, 2004). These sports include surfing, snowboarding, and skateboarding. As Sylvain Lefebvre and Romain Roult (2009) have shown, these practices have gone from being counter-cultural movements to popular movements that have

[2] Hawaiian surfers were seen on the Californian coast as early as the 1880s (Walker, 2011, p. 30), but the practice only took off in the 1950s when the Golden State became "the epicenter of surf media, board manufacturing and design" (Lemarié & Domann, 2019, p. 2).

enabled participants to rediscover nature and the urban space. By doing so, they have transformed individual values and territorialities lived by their practitioners (p. 57). Research has shown how skateboarding has physically appropriated urban spaces (Borden, 2001; Glenney & Mull, 2018; Snyder, 2011), but little to nothing has been said about how the surf lifestyle, through its implementation of music, has also taken over these urban areas by using them as spaces of cultural expression.

Surfing became popular in the 1960s, thanks to cultural productions, such as movies like the iconic *The Endless Summer* by Bruce Brown (1966), or music including hits from The Beach Boys. These productions introduced surfing to places with no waves, and they helped to popularize the lifestyle. Today, surf culture is no longer solely about the act of surfing as a sports practice; it is also about collective and symbolic representations of a set of values associated with surfing (Lefebvre & Roult, 2009; Sayeux, 2005). These representations come to life in the construction of spaces associated with surfing and comprising surf towns like Cocoa Beach.

According to Paul Aho (2014), when the surfing revolution occurred in Florida, during the same period NASA's Kennedy's Space Center sent Neil Armstrong to the Moon, "Space Coast towns were booming—none more than Cocoa Beach, the capital of Space Coast surfing, and arguably of the entire Atlantic Coast as well" (p. 63). Florida surfing lacks scholarly attention because of the peninsula's reputation for not producing good or consistent waves. However, Brevard County is home to legends of surfing, such as Gary Propper, 11-times world champion Kelly Slater, his mentor and air pioneer Matt Kechele, the Hobgood brothers, or a legend-to-be, the young Caroline Marks, who represented the United States in the Olympic Games' first surfing event in Tokyo in 2021. As early as the 1960s, Cocoa Beach became heavily focused on competition, material innovations, and lifestyle promotion, enabling it to develop a strong surf industry maintained today by surf tourism. Prominent surf shop names are now associated with Cocoa Beach. For instance, Ron Jon surf shop (albeit hardcore surfers among my interviewees considered it too "mainstream") is the world's biggest surf shop and a part of an ensemble of institutions that gave the surf town its reputation. Other surf shops, like Catalyst surf shop, cater to the region's core surfers and help it maintain a more "authentic ethos of surfing," defined by my interviewees as "for us, by us." Thus, Cocoa Beach generates at once mainstream and core economies of the surf lifestyle. This dichotomy is observable in the organization of the town (Fig. 2.1). On the one hand, the north part of the town,

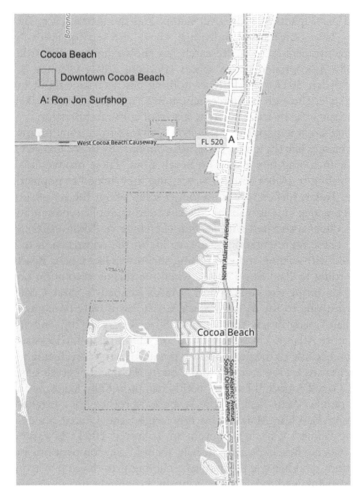

Fig. 2.1 Cocoa Beach. (Source: Map by the author. Base map: Openstreetmap)

where Ron Jon and its mega-complex competitor, Cocoa Beach Surf Company, are located, corresponds to what John Hannigan (1998) calls fantasy city, a highly themed and branded postmodern urban space operated 24 hours-a-day to entertain tourists. On the other hand, the south part of town, its downtown, where Catalyst surf shop, Sun Bum, and other specialty stores are located, constitutes a less scripted and branded

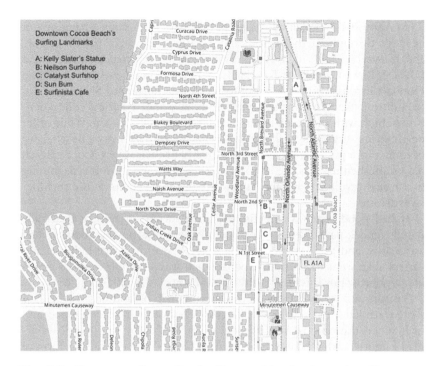

Fig. 2.2 Downtown Cocoa Beach. (Source: Map by the author. Base map: Openstreetmap)

urban space (Fig. 2.2). By creating an intimate concert in the south part of the city, Sonny's Porch benefits from the contrast between the Disneyland of surfing marked by mass-consumerism, artificially themed spaces, and catchy signs and the original surf town marked by a sense of intimacy and "authenticity" built by locals' experience of the beach lifestyle. The "by us, for us" surfers' interpretation of the term "authentic" echoes Connell and Gibson's (2003) idea of authenticity achieved by way of credibility in music and place: "Regions of dynamism and creativity, places perceived to be the origins of novel sounds, become credible as sites of innovation, and subsequently become authentic, as they are increasingly depicted in media and imaginations in relation to music" (p. 44). The same is true with businesses like Sun Bum, which proposes a novel and original approach to sunscreen: a beach lifestyle linked with sports and cultural events managed by credible actors—surfers.

As Aho (2014) explained, "A lot of lives have been shaped hanging out in shops throughout the region, and each has cultivated its own culture and history as well" (p. 84). Innovative surfboard shapers, such as Pat O'Hare, Ricky Carroll, or Tom Neilson, have created new ways of surfing Florida's inconsistent wave conditions (Florida Surfboard Shapers, n.d.). In addition, like Sun Bum, lifestyle brands have added cultural cohesion to a town built with the beach in mind and its corollary: tourism. While other neighboring surf spots, such as Sebastian Inlet south of Cocoa Beach, have become more popular, thanks to the quality of their waves, Cocoa Beach has established itself as the epitome of the surf town from the beginning of the surf revolution because it offered all the elements of the surf lifestyle dream:

It had good waves, competitions, great surfers, dozens of beachside motels, and a party atmosphere like nowhere else on the coast. It had astronauts, and there were watering holes where the space industry and surfers alike went to unwind. Cocoa Beach was a complex mix of family life, highbrow pursuits, and middle-class habits (Aho, 2014, p. 76).

Visitors and locals coexist on this narrow strip of land because of their shared attraction to the beach lifestyle. The locals have developed and maintained the original surf lifestyle characterized by the overall waterman's figure (surfer, boater, fisherman), a Do-It-Yourself (D.I.Y.) form of creativity, and music as an alternative space where a sense of cultural identity is built, as the rest of this chapter shows. It is worth noting that surfing implies notions of localism and territoriality, emphasizing a hierarchical dimension expressed by know-hows, spatial appropriation, and the need to claim socio-cultural belonging (Anderson, 2014; Bennett, 2004; Evers, 2009; Lanagan, 2002; Usher, 2017). In touristic places like Cocoa Beach, surfers—local experts—can reclaim their space through music by building and validating its soundscape. In this process of balancing the "authentic" surf town (the south region built by credible agents of surfing) with the "touristic" one (the north region), "[m]usic [is] probably ubiquitously a part of the tourist experience but as an adjunct to it rather than a rationale for it" (Gibson & Connell, 2005, p. 8). While music's invasion of space only seems to accompany tourists' experience, it also constitutes a forum to voice local surfers' identities.

3 Revisiting Surf Music

Surfing is arguably the only sport that gave its name to a so-called music genre. As I show in my work (Barjolin-Smith, 2020), the notion of genre is problematic when speaking of surf music. For that reason, I call this music a movement that has incorporated various genres over the years, including but not limited to rock and punk in its traditional versions and reggae and country in its local forms. For a mainstream audience, surf music usually relates to The Beach Boys and California's 1960s surfing boom. According to Kent Crowley (2011), surf music started as a revolution in Southern California when local surfers adopted "a new musical democracy: a music of kids, by kids, and for kids [that] was loud, vulgar, primitive, primeval, sexual, and sensual" (p. 5). Crowley (2011) suggested that surf music has existed in resurgent waves as an expression of resistance. While counter-cultural movements, such as punk, associated with surf music over the years, surf music in its iconic definition quickly became a mainstream phenomenon enabling the democratization of Californian surfing culture in the United States and globally. Neither did it represent the diversity and the aesthetics of surfing cultures worldwide, nor did it have continuity.

Americans co-opted surfing[3] and made it theirs through the use and dissemination of this so-called musical genre deemed to have existed in resurrecting waves and which, according to this logic, no longer exists.[4] Consequently, surf music is more accurately defined as a spatiotemporal aesthetic movement constructed locally and globally by surfers and for surfers who make it a part of their lifestyle (Barjolin-Smith, 2020). In the surfing world, music is played during competitions, before and after surf sessions, on surf media, on the beach, in cars, on boats, and in surfers' backyards while barbecuing with friends and family. These musicking contexts are socially and culturally charged since each surfing region in the world is characterized by its language, history, and musical culture. Thus,

---

[3] Colleen McGloin (2005, 2017), who specializes in Indigenous surfing culture, has pointed out that these populations' ancient practices, such as the Hawaiian hula dance or the mele chants, have been removed from their history by way of colonization, expansionism, and cultural appropriation. In her doctoral thesis, she argued that "Idealized and now expropriated, the practices of ancient Hawaiian cultural traditions are excised from their histories" (2005, p. 6).

[4] Blair (1995, 2015) and Crowley (2011) present surf music as such.

Florida's Southern culture and proximity with the Caribbean[5] has influenced its surf music. It is a blend of southern rock, country music, and reggae (Barjolin-Smith, 2018b). Reggae and country share several similarities: they both tell everyday-life stories, are popular and laid-back, use similar instruments. For example, the banjo, an African instrument, was imported in the Caribbean and used in mento, which had an influence on reggae (Conway, 1995; Bradley, 2000). Additionally, both genres are often enjoyed in casual settings, such as bars and backyards, around a beer and barbecue with friends. They are musics[6] that cultivate everyday life, roots, and tradition consciousness. These aspects also correspond to the way surfers conceive musicking in Cocoa Beach. Consequently, surfers have built a type of surf music that matches their subculture's aesthetic requirements and their region's aesthetic heritage. In that respect, the approach to music presented here is similar to Sara Cohen's (2007), who recognized music "as a social and symbolic practice encompassing a diversity of roles and characteristics: music as a culture or way of life distinguished by social and ideological conventions; music as sound; speech and discourse about music; and music as a commodity and industry" (p. 4). Surf music as an aesthetic construction consists of multiple stylistic units displaced, adopted, and transformed into singular subcultural hubs scattered around the surfing world as musical crossovers, which David Brackett (2016) defined as the blending of musical genres (p. 281). As such, it is likely to stem from various local adaptations of seemingly global movements and be "a transgression of social categories" (ibid.) since by mixing different genres, thus different musical cultures, we also blend ethnicities, societies, social status, etc. Surf music can then become punk, reggae, or rock 'n' roll as it matches the cultural and aesthetic tastes and expectations of a regional community of surfers. While it would be erroneous to assert that a whole town could display homogeneous tastes, Motti Regev (2013)

---

[5] As Dave Thompson (2002) pointed out in his encyclopedia of reggae and Caribbean music, "There is no such thing as Caribbean music" (p. vii). Indeed, the Caribbean region is ethnically and culturally heterogeneous because of colonialism and the influence of various European nations on the different islands. In this chapter, the term Caribbean denotes the influence of reggae on Floridian surf music.

[6] The substantive music may be used here with the plural marker-s to indicate music's plurality of genres, scenes, and varieties. This form is encountered in writings on popular music cited in this chapter, like in Bennett and Peterson (2004), and in major works, including Simon Frith's writings to differentiate between music as an art form and the various forms music may take.

and Christopher Small (1998) have shown that individuals develop their sense of taste in relation to one another in a collective effort to reinforce their social identity. As this chapter illustrates, music in the surf town is shared in the private and public spaces so that a collective sense of musicality participates in shaping the town's aesthetics.

4 SONNY'S PORCH CONCERTS

4.1 *Music as Urban Sound*

Cocoa Beach is characterized by the sounds that it generates and that pertain to its specific geographical, social, cultural, and national circumstances. As a beach town, parts of its surface are quieted by the sound of the ocean. As an American town, it is sequenced by the sound of Anglo-American music emanating from public spaces. I confront Craig Gurney's (1999) notion of noise as "a sound which is out of place" (p. 6) to the composer Edgar Varese's definition of music as "organized sound" (Levitin, 2016, p. 2), or more specifically, as a contextually coherent sound. This approach echoes Andy Bennett and Richard Peterson's (2004) concept of scene as a form of musical expression associated with a specific place, generating expectations about this place (p. 3). Music as a spatially coherent sound allows the exploration of the surf town in what Rowland Atkinson (2007) called the "fabric of the urban" (p. 1908).

Furthermore, there is a distinction between the soundscape (a perceptual construct) and the acoustic environment (a physical phenomenon), according to which the former exists through the latter's perception (Brooks et al., 2014, p. 32). A soundscape's acoustic distinction makes a place sound different and unique, giving it a subjective meaning to local and transitory populations. In the surf town's soundscape, music played in public spaces has become one of the urban sounds expected by local communities to validate their collective taste and accompany their daily lives within their town. Strolling through Cocoa Beach, one can hear Anglo-American music coming from the stores, the open restaurants and bars, the cars, etc. As Regev (2013) has highlighted, these songs played in the communal space "set the city's public musical soundscape" (p. 159). They become associated with this particular place as they build its singular aura and impact individual and collective memory. In the surf town, which has built its identity and its economy on tourism and the surf industry, music reinforces the surf lifestyle and serves as the town's original soundtrack.

In Cocoa Beach, successful businesses—surf shops, bars, or restaurants—have promoted their region's beach culture and entertained the look and feel of the city as a laid-back surf town through their merchandising of the culture. However, Cocoa Beach is a resort town and a residential area at once, so businesses cannot simply focus on catering to tourists. Indeed, surfers live and work there, broadcasting and sharing their music in the public space. This music has a social function since it is associated with all the collective aspects of the surf lifestyle implemented in the surf town (including, going out with friends, participating in concerts, watching competitions from the beach, etc.). Sun Bum's implementation of music illustrates how the urban setting is used to construct a sense of collective aesthetic identity.

4.2   Private Sounds in the Public Space

One might find it odd and unusual for a sunscreen company to coordinate musical events and associate with D.J.s. However, strategizing to become a part of the surf town's historical and ideological narratives has proven successful for long-lasting businesses in Cocoa Beach. Sun Bum is a so-called lifestyle brand. It sells products associated with a way of living—the beach and surf lifestyles—and as such, it promotes every aspect of the surf lifestyle, including music. Sun Bum's marketing strategy is based on the Big Three's (Rip Curl, Quiksilver, Billabong) strategy to distinguish between core and mainstream but cater to both consumer types (Stranger, 2013, pp. 67–68). In line with the Big Three's surf industry standards, employees are surfers who do not hesitate (and are even encouraged) to close the office whenever waves are in the forecast. While this marketing strategy helps cultivate the myth of authenticity, in effect, Sun Bum's founders have hired surfers to develop and promote the brand since its inception in 2010.[7]

The company has dedicated its space to the hosting of mini-concerts called Sonny's Porch. Sonny is the name of the brand's gorilla mascot. The

---

[7] I have observed Sun Bum since its establishment in 2010, and I have kept in touch with its founders, which has given me an in-depth understanding of the brand's culture. The American multinational company, S.C Johnson, acquired Sun Bum in 2019. Despite the obvious risk of falling into a strong corporate culture, so far, Sun Bum's new C.E.O. has fostered the brand's core culture by promoting a bottom-up approach to leadership. For instance, she has visited local Sun Bum representatives to gain knowledge from their experience as surfers and promoters of the brand.

casual Floridian beach lifestyle has inspired the look and feel of the brand. The original office is an old traditional Florida house open to the public. In the backyard, there is a wooden porch hidden from the street by Areca palm trees where the concerts take place. At the porch entrance, there is a shower that surfers or beachgoers can use on their way back from the beach. According to the office manager, a surfer himself, the concerts' rationale was that surfers enjoy gathering around a beer and some music after a surf session, so Sun Bum wanted to reproduce this private backyard party experience for the public. Goffman's (1956) concept of decorum (briefly summed up as public appearance and display of specific cultural values) can help illustrate Sun Bum's role in portraying the town through Sonny's Porch concerts. Sun Bum's decorum pertains to its employees who maintain it and allow the brand to fit Cocoa Beach by displaying expected values, thus giving it a favorable image. One of the ways Sun Bum can build its image is through Sonny's Porch. These concerts organized by surfer-employees allow Sun Bum to perform as an "authentic" agent of the surfing world as they imitate a real-life surfers' ritual: the post-surf gathering of friends around beer and music. The audience does not see the organization it takes to have this impromptu-looking feast, this "we invited our musician friends over to play for free" feast in their backyard. The result is credible, which can only be achieved because of employees' insiders' experience of the surfing world. Unlike standard artistic performances, no wall separates backstage and frontstage since the concerts occur at the office, and the audience is allowed outside and inside the premises. Participants enter through the back porch—not the front porch visible from the main street—which gives them a sense of closeness and privileged intimacy with the agents of the surfing world. As music goes beyond the property's borders, it allows them to assert their surf culture's prominence in the town.

Indeed, the concerts hosted on the porch are not acoustic, and technology is used to amplify the sounds that cross the property's limits and resonate into the streets in the middle of the afternoon. Anyone hearing the music from the street is welcome to stop by and participate since Sonny's Porch is free and open to the public (Fig. 2.3. Sonny's Porch Concert). With Sonny's Porch, Sun Bum allows music to be produced in an unusual setting—an office's backyard—and shared with anyone wanting to enjoy it. The music played is not a recording, which would not occupy the physical space and affect passersby. It is a concert—a conversation between musicians and listeners, between those who make culture and those who

Fig. 2.3 Sonny's Porch Concert. View from the street. Passersby. (Source: Photography taken by the author)

consume it. The very nature of a concert is to be unique since music is played live as opposed to being recorded and repeated. Accordingly, the sounds that shape the space around the office, and punctually in Cocoa Beach, are original acts produced for and by the city dwellers in keeping with its singular setting.

Besides, the majority of concerts in Cocoa Beach do not occur inside; they are in the open for all to hear. As Attali (1985) pointed out, concerts have always been charged with a sense of power. The form of concerts, paying in concert halls or free and outdoor, represents power or popularity. Sonny's Porch concerts are a mix of free and in the open (thus popular) and intimate and in the know[8] (thus exclusive). While the events are a strategy to promote the brand's cool and maintain its "authenticity," I suggest that these free concerts implemented by the subculture's agents

---

[8] The concerts are not advertised. Instead, the office manager invites locals to participate while the rest of the audience comprises passersby.

provide a pause in the surf town's commodification[9] during which people stop producing and consuming purchased goods to gather as a community and share an experience within their town as a cultural space, not as a commodity-production space. Yet, the concerts engage a power relationship between surfers and the city's normative attributes as they change the town's working rhythm. With them, surfers reclaim their right to make noise in the public space without conventional borders: an office space in the middle of the old town, not a concert-dedicated space. During the concerts, the street's noise no longer invades the private space, but the private surf sound invades the streets. Through this model, Sun Bum imposes its music on the town and makes the population aware of their presence and cool. In this process, surfers, and through them, surf-related businesses, take possession of the public space through the musical events they organize and participate in.

It is worth clarifying that surf music has not modified the town's physical structure; neither have surfers physically been using the infrastructures as skateboarders would. However, they have performed an appropriation of the public space by claiming it as a place of socio-cultural expression and experience. Indeed, as Cohen (2007) suggested, "The city is not simply a place where music happens, or a container or inert setting for music activity. Instead, music can be conceived as contributing to the making or 'social production' of the city" (p. 35). Thus, while a town's architecture and infrastructures constitute its look, its cultural practices capture its feel, or as Connell and Gibson (2003) explained, places and sounds are connected in "a process of mythologising place in which unique, locally experienced social, economic and political circumstances are somehow 'captured' within music" (p. 14). Surfing and its related practices, such as

---

[9] In keeping with the notions of authenticity and credibility, the events temporarily break away from capitalism because core lifestyle sports participants/employees engage their credibility in making these events. They fight to protect their vision and their subculture within the company. For instance, as Sun Bum expanded after being purchased by S.C. Johnson in 2019, these agents became the gatekeepers of the brand's original ethos. One surfer and skateboarder who had worked for Sun Bum before its S.C.J's acquisition explained to another staff member coming from the beauty world and transitioning to a skateboarding brand that the lack of respect and humility she had displayed in regards to these subcultures and their agents while working for Sun Bum would backfire. He told her, "skateboarders actually live this, and it is harder to break into than surfing, so you can't just tell people what to do and not listen to what they have to say." Thus, the sliding scale of capitalism represents how the lifestyle sports agents manufacture their activity, allowing their lifestyle dreams to take precedence.

36   A. BARJOLIN-SMITH

musicking, "affect the aural character of segments of the city" (Atkinson, 2007, p. 1909). Surfers stage their practice through physical appearance and their musicking, thus enriching the urban space with their culture. They go beyond the visual affirmation of their culture marked by their bodies, and they transcend the urban space—public and private—with their music. Music marks surfers' symbolic territory as a liminal zone of socialization where non-surfers are welcome to explore what surfers are willing to share about their culture. As Daniel André Fernandes Paiva (2019) showed, "artistic practices, by producing sonic first impressions, alter the way individuals perceive urban space, and consequently, how individuals appropriate and contribute toward the formation of territories in urban space" (p. 1). Sun Bum contributes to the towns' sonic portrayal with its open-air concerts and creates aural surfers' territories characterized by a limited musical genre scope.

5   THE SURF TOWN'S GLOCAL SOUNDSCAPE

The Sub Bum office manager in Cocoa Beach is in charge of finding artists that he, as a surfer, would like to see. The artists who perform at Sonny's Porch can be from anywhere in the world as long as they satisfy the subjective construction of the community's surf experience, which, according to local surfers, has to promote a "fun and positive" approach to the lifestyle (much influenced by the Caribbean culture broadly defined).[10] During my participant observation, I attended concerts of artists from diverse musical and geographical backgrounds, such as Hawaiian reggae (Mike Love), Barbadian reggae (Collie Budz), Californian psychedelic rock (The Growlers), Floridian garage rock (Jacuzzi Boys), Hawaiian surf rock (Donavon Frankenreiter), among others. Favored genres consistently spanned from rock to reggae, representing this Floridian surf town's geographical and cultural setting. Having a sense of the type of music played and shared in the public space helps investigate the formation and function of surfing music in the shaping of the urban space. From a sociocultural standpoint, concerts temporally set up the sounds of the surf

---

[10] My research has highlighted that Floridian surfers tend to promote a less aggressive approach to surfing than some of their counterparts, like Californians or Brazilians. During my ethnographic research, interviewees situated Florida "in the heart of the Caribbean." They often used the words "fun" and "positive" to describe their lifestyle and the music they envisioned for it.

provide a pause in the surf town's commodification[9] during which people stop producing and consuming purchased goods to gather as a community and share an experience within their town as a cultural space, not as a commodity-production space. Yet, the concerts engage a power relationship between surfers and the city's normative attributes as they change the town's working rhythm. With them, surfers reclaim their right to make noise in the public space without conventional borders: an office space in the middle of the old town, not a concert-dedicated space. During the concerts, the street's noise no longer invades the private space, but the private surf sound invades the streets. Through this model, Sun Bum imposes its music on the town and makes the population aware of their presence and cool. In this process, surfers, and through them, surf-related businesses, take possession of the public space through the musical events they organize and participate in.

It is worth clarifying that surf music has not modified the town's physical structure; neither have surfers physically been using the infrastructures as skateboarders would. However, they have performed an appropriation of the public space by claiming it as a place of socio-cultural expression and experience. Indeed, as Cohen (2007) suggested, "The city is not simply a place where music happens, or a container or inert setting for music activity. Instead, music can be conceived as contributing to the making or 'social production' of the city" (p. 35). Thus, while a town's architecture and infrastructures constitute its look, its cultural practices capture its feel, or as Connell and Gibson (2003) explained, places and sounds are connected in "a process of mythologising place in which unique, locally experienced social, economic and political circumstances are somehow 'captured' within music" (p. 14). Surfing and its related practices, such as

---

[9] In keeping with the notions of authenticity and credibility, the events temporarily break away from capitalism because core lifestyle sports participants/employees engage their credibility in making these events. They fight to protect their vision and their subculture within the company. For instance, as Sun Bum expanded after being purchased by S.C. Johnson in 2019, these agents became the gatekeepers of the brand's original ethos. One surfer and skateboarder who had worked for Sun Bum before its S.C.J's acquisition explained to another staff member coming from the beauty world and transitioning to a skateboarding brand that the lack of respect and humility she had displayed in regards to these subcultures and their agents while working for Sun Bum would backfire. He told her, "skateboarders actually live this, and it is harder to break into than surfing, so you can't just tell people what to do and not listen to what they have to say." Thus, the sliding scale of capitalism represents how the lifestyle sports agents manufacture their activity, allowing their lifestyle dreams to take precedence.

musicking, "affect the aural character of segments of the city" (Atkinson, 2007, p. 1909). Surfers stage their practice through physical appearance and their musicking, thus enriching the urban space with their culture. They go beyond the visual affirmation of their culture marked by their bodies, and they transcend the urban space—public and private—with their music. Music marks surfers' symbolic territory as a liminal zone of socialization where non-surfers are welcome to explore what surfers are willing to share about their culture. As Daniel André Fernandes Paiva (2019) showed, "artistic practices, by producing sonic first impressions, alter the way individuals perceive urban space, and consequently, how individuals appropriate and contribute toward the formation of territories in urban space" (p. 1). Sun Bum contributes to the towns' sonic portrayal with its open-air concerts and creates aural surfers' territories characterized by a limited musical genre scope.

5   THE SURF TOWN'S GLOCAL SOUNDSCAPE

The Sub Bum office manager in Cocoa Beach is in charge of finding artists that he, as a surfer, would like to see. The artists who perform at Sonny's Porch can be from anywhere in the world as long as they satisfy the subjective construction of the community's surf experience, which, according to local surfers, has to promote a "fun and positive" approach to the lifestyle (much influenced by the Caribbean culture broadly defined).[10] During my participant observation, I attended concerts of artists from diverse musical and geographical backgrounds, such as Hawaiian reggae (Mike Love), Barbadian reggae (Collie Budz), Californian psychedelic rock (The Growlers), Floridian garage rock (Jacuzzi Boys), Hawaiian surf rock (Donavon Frankenreiter), among others. Favored genres consistently spanned from rock to reggae, representing this Floridian surf town's geographical and cultural setting. Having a sense of the type of music played and shared in the public space helps investigate the formation and function of surfing music in the shaping of the urban space. From a sociocultural standpoint, concerts temporally set up the sounds of the surf

---

[10] My research has highlighted that Floridian surfers tend to promote a less aggressive approach to surfing than some of their counterparts, like Californians or Brazilians. During my ethnographic research, interviewees situated Florida "in the heart of the Caribbean." They often used the words "fun" and "positive" to describe their lifestyle and the music they envisioned for it.

town—its soundscape—to define the city. Therefore, in Atkinson's words, the soundscape is "socially organizing" (p. 1907).

As Cohen (2007) suggested, by focusing on the implementation and the content produced during concerts, it is possible to explore:

General trends within one particular city and thus in studying the global within the local, considering how global trends are mediated by local (and also national) socio-economic circumstances, as well as by the social and ideological conventions that inform popular music production and consumption and genre-based cultures or scenes (p. 4).

Even though there is a diversity of musical genres played throughout the town, a trend is noticeable, which matches the programming of Sonny's Porch. It is a type of music that is perceived as "generating happiness" and "maintaining a laid-back aura" more so than a fast pace or aggressive one. While music is not in itself positive or laid-back, it can convey these ideas and represent them (Barjolin-Smith, 2018b, p. 45). In his work on music and the brain, Daniel J. Levitin (2016) showed that music could also alter our moods depending on the melody, the rhythm, the harmonies, the timbre, the lyrics, the context to which it is associated, and a community of listeners' shared interpretation of it. As Frith (1996a) pointed out, "while music may be shaped by the people who first make and use it, as experience it has a life of its own" (p. 109). Indeed, one female surfer, singer, and D.J. explained that people in general and surfers, in particular, gravitate around reggae in the Cocoa Beach area. For her, "the energy of the music is very laid-back. It's kind of like, you know, I think living by the beach, we don't have that bustle and hustle of the city here. It's a small town. We've got that laid-back kind of island-style." She and most of my interviewees viewed reggae as happy and laid-back music that they associated with the archetypal Caribbean lifestyle and culture, thus with the values of reggae. Their interpretation of the music highlights their shared sensibilities, which echoes the notion of scene discussed by Bennett and Peterson (2004). Broadly defined, scenes aggregate music producers, makers, and consumers around their common tastes, and they can be local, trans-local, or virtual. The reggae scene is trans-local as it is "connected with groups of kindred spirits many miles away" (ibid., p. 9). These communities share a common representation of what reggae means to them. I interviewed a surfer and D.J. specialized in reggae, who explained his interpretation of reggae values as "very deeply rooted in a positive message. It's about love, or it's about fun." Therefore, while musics that constitute surf music in Florida, like reggae, do not necessarily originate from Florida, they are blended in the town's character. Hence, a sense of *Floridaness* is successfully combined with the global sounds of surf music to allow the emergence of a soundscape culturally validated by the locals (Barjolin-Smith, 2018b). Besides Sonny's Porch, much of the music played in the town's public space is not from the United States, so musical textures have been imported and included in the local surf music. Regev (2013) claimed that "textures have the potential to usher in new modes of individual and collective experiences, alter the physical reality of public spaces, and in general affect cultural performance at the individual and collective levels" (p. 160). For example, the inclusion of reggae in surf music has also led to adopting its characteristic colors (green, yellow, red) and one interpretation of its philosophy of life. Many surfers from Cocoa Beach wear these colors or support an iteration of the reggae-related interpretation of the Rastafarian doctrine. Reggae in Florida is not perceived as the music of the have-nots; it is island music. It is reggae inspired by an Anglo-American condensed history of the genre in the figure of Bob Marley because "For many people, Bob Marley *is* reggae" (Bradley, 2000, p. 397). Moreover, for my interviewees, Rastafarianism was not necessarily the so-called cult or celebration of a free African nation let by Emperor Haile Selassie I, "a universal black role model" (Bradley, 2000, p. 64) by its Caribbean diaspora; it was an Anglo-American interpretation praising values of love, respect, and brotherhood. Two D.J.s working in collaboration with Sun Bum promoted this vision along with the intrinsic relationship between reggae and surfing. The first one deejayed on a local surf radio called Endless Summer Radio and played reggae on a program titled Sun Bum Positive Sunday ("Endless Summer Radio," n.d.); the other one, whose label named Kulcha Shok specialized in reggae culture, sponsored local and national surf events ("Kulcha Shok," n.d.). These two D.J.s occupy public space and share it with other musical genres. Accordingly, the presence of foreign musics, such as traditional reggae, and local musics, such as country, makes Cocoa Beach share "much aesthetic common ground with those of other urban settings in the world" (Regev, 2013, p. 171). The incorporation of the global into the local and the connection of various localities into the configuration of the global is what Robertson (1995) called glocalization (p. 31). The definition of surf music proposed here illustrates this notion as it constitutes a glocal soundscape made of stylistic sub-units, such as rock or reggae, that can be recognized by any listener—surfer or non-surfer—and appropriated (Barjolin-Smith, 2018b).

As Bennett and Peterson (2004) highlighted regarding jazz players, "where they perform affects what they perform" (p. 19). The music played in Sonny's Porch is affected by the setting and the place; however, a genre remains within a porous scope that listeners can identify and relate to regardless of the variations from place to place. Regev (2013) argued that "[l]ocal urban musical environments thus become global ... soundscapes, places where one feels local and global at the very same time" (p. 171). Surfers and surf towns are glocal because of the movements and hybridization of cultures. Thus, people's musical knowledge has given them the ability to belong to the local and the global at once through and thanks to their urban space. An important nuance lies in the term glocal that has to do with the global character of a phenomenon built in its singular local iterations, as various communities appropriate it. In that regard, a comparison of the surfing world with Hodkinson's (2004) study of goths helps highlight surfing and surf music's glocal nature. Localism and territoriality are recurring tropes in the surfing world. Thus, unlike goths, who would want to meet goths from different countries, surfing is more territorial and the transnational community much bigger and competitive. That said, in Cocoa Beach, the surfing community is very tightly knit with the local non-surfing population as their culture dovetails into the beach lifestyle. Where the goths seem to be fairly consistent from one locality to the next (ibid., p. 135), there are many variables to consider with surfing and surf music, such as regional rivalries and approaches to surfing. For instance, California and Florida differ in terms of history, practice, and image. Thus, surfing is trans-local in terms of fundamental commonalities, but it has developed rhizomatically (Barjolin-Smith, 2020), generating singular practices and local identities. As my interviewees concurred, Cocoa Beach surfers would be "less territorial" and overall "less aggressive" than Californian surfers. They also prefer reggae over a prevailing metal scene on the west coast. Another contrast between goths and surfers that helps understand surfing culture's specificity is that goths may shop in local non-specialist stores, but surfers have a "for us, by us" mentality that supports the consumption of locally produced and branded goods manifest through their displaying of brand items that label them at least as surfers, and at best, as local surfers belonging to a specific community.[11] Sun Bum learned to draw from local cultural resources to cater to local

---

[11] Surfers may recognize kooks (someone posing as a surfer or a *wannabe*) by their attire. Kooks would wear the wrong brands like a Salt Life t-shirt.

surfers and Cocoa Beach dwellers. As Deborah Leslie and Norma M. Rantisi (2011) showed, "The producers of cultural commodities draw on place-specific resources (ranging from infrastructure to artists) and place-based images to imbue commodities with a distinct aesthetic quality, a feature which can serve as a basis for competitive advantage" (p. 1774). This is what Sun Bum did when it partnered with local D.J.s and relied on its employees' decorum to reinforce its credibility and establish its symbolic authenticity through Sonny's Porch concerts.

6   ORGANIZATION: SPACE APPROPRIATION AND AESTHETIC IDENTITY

As Cocoa Beach's glocal soundscape illustrates, while music is created within a specific geo-cultural context, it is inextricably mobile and does not spread uniformly around the globe. Simon Frith (1996a) suggested that music may mean one thing in its birthplace and be experienced differently in other locations (p. 109). Musics are domesticated and help define the cultural threshold of various local communities, such as the Cocoa Beach community of surfers. The corporeality of music (as texture and invader of body and space through its effects on them) aggregates those who live with it into belonging communities. Membership in these communities amounts to a collective aesthetic identity built by the repetitive encounter with music that is or becomes familiar and appreciated, which is what Frith (1996b) called "performing rites" (p. 273). These rites or musical commonalities shape the cultural life of the town as well as its collective identity. In other words, the surf town of Cocoa Beach has been shaped and modified as a cultural object by the materialization of sounds consisting of a blend of reggae music and other local genres, such as rock and country music. The resulting sound—a blend of urban and beach noises and musical sounds—functions as an agent in the town's aesthetic construction. As the town becomes associated with this sound—its musical scene—a circle of practices is implemented in which locals create and expect specific patterns. According to Gibson and Connell (2005), the associations between sound and place "combined with music's powerful, emotive role in acts of consumption, create patterns of demands that translate into new local cultural economies, as discourses of 'authenticity' and 'distinctiveness' are mobilised across markets at a variety of scales, and become means of transforming places" (p. 14). Through Sonny's Porch concerts, Sun Bum has played an influential role in creating a new local cultural economy and singularizing the surf town's cultural practices and identity. Thus, they have engaged in what I call surfanization, a process in which surfing appropriates the urban space and shapes the town's aesthetic identity—the experience of a space built as an American-Southern-Caribbean-influenced surf town.

What conveys its aesthetic identity to the surf town is the repetition of certain musical patterns or musical dimensions that have become culturally ingrained in the canvas of the town because of the sense of memory they have built in association with this specific urban setting. Music has played a role in the sense of belonging of individuals working collectively to mark a local identity within the town. By triggering social interactions within spaces not usually dedicated to concerts, Sun Bum has provided surfers with an opportunity to shape the aesthetics of their town through the sharing of their musical influences, and surfers have provided Sun Bum with the credibility to host Sonny's Porch concerts.

7   Concluding Thoughts

The surf town's location and related socio-cultural activities largely influence its identity. However, city dwellers can alter or refine a surf town's identity by impacting its soundscape with their music. By doing so, they participate in constructing the town's cultural economy. Like Sun Bum's employees, these expert agents of the urban space rely on their knowledge of the appropriate culture and the place's resources to concretize their vision of the surf town through their musicking. They assert their credibility by showcasing surfing culture and anchoring it into their urban environment. Thus, concerts have become a forum where surfers can voice their vision of an authentic surfing community's identity instead of the mainstream image of surfing spread through archetypal representations of surfing, epitomized by bands like The Beach Boys.

Music is complex to grasp because of its multiple aspects intertwined in a global web of cultural practices and sonic experiences. However, by examining the effects of music on the urban environment, it is possible to see past its ungraspable nature as a materialization of the human mind. The corporeality of music has allowed individuals and communities to mark their aesthetic identities within singular cultural spaces inscribed in a global network of cultural identities. For Frith (1996b), music "gives us a way of being in the world, a way of making sense of it" (p. 272), and while music is shared worldwide, its diversity is cultivated in the form of musical hybrids that shape and renew spaces, as illustrated in the surfanization of Cocoa Beach.

REFERENCES

Aho, P. (2014). *Surfing Florida: A photographic history*. University Press of Florida.

Anderson, J. (2014). Surfing between the local and the global: Identifying spatial divisions in surfing practice. *Transactions of the Institute of British Geographers, 39*(2), 237–249. https://doi.org/10.1111/tran.12018

Atkinson, R. (2007). Ecology of sound: The sonic order of urban space. *Urban Studies, 44*(10), 1905–1917. https://doi.org/10.1080/00420980701471901

Attali, J. (1985). *Noise: The political economy of music* (10th ed.). University of Minnesota Press.

Barjolin-Smith, A. (2018a). *Ethno-esthétique du surf en Floride: Impact des liens entre surf et musique sur les marquages identitaires*. Doctoral thesis, Université Paul Valéry, Montpellier 3.

Barjolin-Smith, A. (2018b). Surfing through music: Sharing the surf lifestyle on a reggae frequency. *Riffs: Experimental Writing on Popular Music, 2*(2).

Barjolin-Smith, A. (2020). *Ethno-aesthetics of surf in Florida: Surf, musicking and identity marking*. Palgrave Macmillan.

Bennett, R. (2004). *The surfer's mind: The complete, practical guide to surf psychology*. Griffin Press.

Bennett, A., & Peterson, A. R. (2004). *Music scenes: Local, translocal and virtual*. Vanderbilt University Press.

Blair, J. (1995). *The illustrated discography of surf music 1961–1965* (3rd ed.). Popular Culture Ink.

Blair, J. (2015). *Southern California surf music, 1960–1966*. Arcadia Publishing.

Borden, I. (2001). *Skateboarding, space and the city: Architecture and the body*. Berg.

Brackett, D. (2016). *Categorizing sound: Genre and twentieth-century popular music*. University of California Press.

Bradley, L. (2000). *This is reggae music: The story of Jamaica's music*. Grove Press.

Brooks, B. M., Schulte-Fortkamp, B., Voigt, K. S., & Case, A. U. (2014). Exploring our sonic environment through soundscape research & theory. *Acoustics Today, 10*(1), 30–40. https://doi.org/10.1121/1.4870174

Brown, B. (1966). *The endless summer* [Film]. Aviva International.

Coëffé, V. (2010). La plage, fabrique d'une touristi(cité) idéale. *L'Information géographique, 74*(3), 51–68. https://doi.org/10.3917/lig.743.0051

Coëffé, V. (2014). *Hawaï: La fabrique d'un espace touristique*. Presses Universitaires de Rennes.

Cohen, S. (2007). *Decline, renewal and the city in popular music culture: Beyond the Beatles.* Ashgate.

Connell, J., & Gibson, C. (2003). *Sound tracks: Popular music, identity and place* (2nd ed.). Routledge.

Conway, C. (1995). *African banjo echoes in Appalachia: A study of folk traditions.* University of Tennessee Press.

Crowley, K. (2011). *Surf beat: Rock'n'roll's forgotten revolution.* Backbeat Book.

Endless Summer Radio. (n.d.). Retrieved April 9, 2019, from http://endlesssummerradio.com/

Evers, C. (2009). 'The Point': Surfing, geography and a sensual life of men and masculinity on the Gold Coast. *Australia. Social & Cultural Geography, 10*(8), 893–908. https://doi.org/10.1080/14649360903305783

Florida Surfboard Shapers. (n.d.). Retrieved April 9, 2019, from http://www.boardcave.com/surfboard-shapers/usa/east-coast/florida/

Frith, S. (1996a). Music and identity. In S. Hall & P. DuGay (Eds.), *Cultural identity.* Sage Publications.

Frith, S. (1996b). *Performing rites.* Harvard University Press.

Gibson, C., & Connell, J. (2005). *Music and tourism: On the road again.* Channel View Publications.

Glenney, B., & Mull, S. (2018). Skateboarding and the ecology of urban space. *Journal of Sport and Social Issues, 42*(6), 437–453. https://doi.org/10.1177/0193723518800525

Goffman, E. (1956). *The presentation of self in everyday life.* University of Edinburgh.

Gurney, C. (1999). Rattle and hum: Gendered accounts of noise as a pollutant: An aural sociology of work and home. Paper presented to the *Health and Safety Authority Conference*, York, April.

Hannigan, J. (1998). *Fantasy city: Pleasure and profit in the postmodern metropolis.* Routledge.

Hodkinson, P. (2004). Translocal connections in the goth scene. In A. Bennett & A. R. Peterson (Eds.), *Music scenes: Local, translocal, and virtual.* Vanderbilt University Press.

Kulcha Shok Muzik. (n.d.). Retrieved April 9, 2019, from http://kulchashok.com/

Lanagan, D. (2002). Surfing in the third millennium: Commodyfing the visual argot. *The Australian Journal of Anthropology, 13*(3), 283–291.

Lefebvre, S., & Roult, R. (2009). Les nouveaux territoires du surf dans la ville. *Téoros: Revue de recherche en tourisme, 28*(2), 55. https://doi.org/10.7202/1024807ar

Lemarié, J., & Domann, V. (2019). Branding Huntington Beach, Surf City USA®: Visitors, residents, and businesses. *Loisir et Société / Society and Leisure, 42*(3), 401–419. https://doi.org/10.1080/07053436.2019.1681805

44   A. BARJOLIN-SMITH

Leslie, D., & Rantisi, N. M. (2011). Creativity and place in the evolution of a cultural industry: The case of Cirque du Soleil. *Urban Studies, 48*(9), 1771–1787. https://doi.org/10.1177/0042098010377475

Levitin, J. D. (2016). *The world in six songs: How the musical brain created human nature.* Dutton.

McGloin, C. (2005). *Surfing nation(s)—Surfing country(s).* Doctoral Thesis, University of Wollongong, Wollongong.

McGloin, C. (2017). Indigenous surfing: Pedagogy, pleasure, and decolonial practice. In D. Zavalza Hough-Snee & A. Sotelo Eastman (Eds.), *The critical surf studies reader* (pp. 196–213). Duke University Press.

Paiva, D. A. F. (2019). *Urban sound: Territories, affective atmospheres, and politics.* Doctoral Thesis, University of Lisbon, Lisbon.

Parrish, A. E., Field, A. C., & Harrell, G. L. (2001). *Merritt Island and Cocoa Beach.* Arcadia Publishing.

Regev, M. (2013). *Pop-rock music: Aesthetic cosmopolitanism in late modernity.* Polity Press.

Robertson, R. (1995). Glocalization: Time-space and homogeneity-heterogeneity. In M. Featherstone, S. Lash, & R. Robertson (Eds.), *Global modernities* (pp. 25–44). Sage.

Sayeux, A.-S. (2005). *Surfeur, l'être au monde: Analyse socio-anthropologique de la culture de surfeurs, entre accords et déviance.* Doctoral thesis, Université de Rennes 2.

Schafer, R. M. (1977). *The tuning of the world.* Random House.

Small, C. (1998). *Musicking: The meaning of performing and listening.* Wesleyan University Press.

Snyder, B. C. (2011). *A secret history of the ollie* (2nd ed.). Black Salt Press.

Stranger, M. (2013). Surface and substructure: Beneath surfing's commodified surface. In *The consumption and representation of lifestyle sports* (pp. 61–78). Routledge.

Thompson, D. (2002). *Reggae and Caribbean music.* Backbeat Book.

Usher, L. E. (2017). "Foreign locals": Transnationalism, expatriates, and surfer identity in Costa Rica. *Journal of Sport and Social Issues, 41*(3), 212–238.v. https://doi.org/10.1177/0193723517705542

Walker, I. H. (2011). *Waves of resistance: Surfing and history in twentieth-century Hawai'i.* University of Hawaii Press.

Wheaton, B. (Ed.). (2004). *Understanding lifestyle sports: Consumption, identity and difference.* Routledge.

CHAPTER 3

Street Piano: An Instrument of Urban Change

Alenka Barber-Kersovan

Abstract During the last decades the growing importance of culture in urban policy includes a noticeable accumulation of festivals. Next to major spectacles such as Olympic games (festivalization) also smaller size events are staged which aim predominantly at recipients' emotions and must not necessarily have a direct economic or financial spillover effect (eventification). They are carried out by a large range of stakeholders whereby next to traditional players with their top-down policies the experience economy put forth also some new agents, such as bottom-up cultural initiatives, social associations, and artists.

This is also the case with the touring installation *Street Piano – Play Me, I'm Yours* discussed in this chapter. The project is designed by the British artist Luke Jerram and implies that several artistically painted pianos are put into the urban space to be used and played by anybody who feels inspired. The aim of the project is to induce a "positive change within the city" by "claiming ownership of [the] urban landscape" through

---

A. Barber-Kersovan (✉)
Institute for Sociology and Cultural Organisation, Leuphana University, Lüneburg, Germany
e-mail: alenka.barber-kersovan@leuphana.de

© The Author(s), under exclusive license to Springer Nature   45
Singapore Pte Ltd. 2024
S. Guillard et al. (eds.), *New Geographies of Music 2*, Geographies of Media, https://doi.org/10.1007/978-981-97-2072-9_3

musicing. Till 2020 some 2000 pianos have been installed in over 60 cities with an estimated reach of 20 million people which makes it one of the most successful contemporary projects.

The method applied for this chapter can be associated with research techniques such as digital ethnography and Internet ethnography, though the Internet has been deployed predominantly as a data-gathering instrument. The interpretation of the project followed the hermeneutical content analysis, whereby the explanatory lens focused on the event character of the project, the role of the artist Luke Jerram as an agent of the urban revitalization, his cooperation with the urban growth coalition and the takeover of his project idea by other stakeholders.

Keywords Luke Jerram • Street Piano • Artist-led urban revitalization • Public art • Culturalization of cities

> *Street performance has the capacity to create a sense of place and to create positive change within a city. Where there's music and entertainment on the streets, you'll find a city that's open to creative possibilities—a place that thinks and cares about citizens.*
> —Luke Jerram

1   INTRODUCTION

1.1   *Festivalization and Culturalization of Cities*

During the last decades, a new "centrality of culture in urban policy" (Richards & Palmer, 2010, p. 24) is notified. This growing importance of culture is due to aspects such as the stimulation of the economic growth, the regeneration of de-industrialized quarters, the strengthening of social inclusion, and the image design of the rapidly expanding municipalities. Being loaded with meanings from other fields of the social, economic, and political life, cultural events seized to be just a matter of culture and became a vital part of the development and the revitalization of the rapidly changing urban landscape. They are believed to contribute to the solving of broader socio-economic problems generated outside the actual culture as well as to create wealth from cultural goods and activities.

Different strategies have been applied to turn these assumptions into practice. The first one was prompted by the spectacular architecture based on the model of the *Guggenheim Museum* Frank Gehry designed for a neglected neighborhood in the Basque city of Bilbao. Since this iconic building gave the region an enormous boost (Bilbao effect), the concept was imitated countless times and resulted in a global building boom of new museums, opera houses, and concert halls (Barber-Kersovan, 2021). They are set in the service of city branding (*Sydney Opera House*) and instrumentalized to foster tourism and attract capital and qualified labor on a national and international scale.

The second aspect is the fostering of "creativity" as conceptualized by Richard Florida (2002) and Charles Landry (2008). An important issue represented here is the connection to the so-called creative industries. This term refers to the cultural production with an economic dimension carried out by small businesses from different aesthetic branches. They tend to settle down in the immediate spatial vicinity to inspire cooperation, generate new ideas, and develop them into marketable products. Mostly situated in the run-down parts of de-industrialized cities, they contribute to gentrification and form together with cafes, boutiques, and galleries attractive "creative quarters" with an urban atmosphere (Barber-Kersovan, 2007).

Another key point concerns the festivalization of urban policies as formulated by Hartmut Häußermann and Walter Siebel (1993). This term refers to the noticeable accumulation of festivals and other major events in the recent decades on a global scale (Betz et al., 2011; Bittner, 2002; Hitzler, 2011; Smith, 2016). As the term festivalization is mostly used with regard to economically significant mega-spectacles such as World exhibitions and Olympic games (comp. also Richards & Palmer, 2010), Doreen Jakob proposed the term "eventification" for smaller size events.[1] She defined events as a "deliberate organisation of a heightened emotional and aesthetic experience at a disintegration time and space" (Jakob, 2013, p. 448) which aim predominantly at recipients' emotions and must not necessarily have a direct economic or financial spillover effect.

This understanding was adopted also for the present chapter, discussing the event character of the *Play Me, I'm Yours Project* and its derivates and their role for the production and revitalization of the urban space.

---

[1] Andrew Smith (2016, p. 53) speaks in this connection about eventisation whereby Richards and Palmer (2010) prefer the spelling eventization. Also, the semantic connotations of the more specific processes of eventification, eventalisation, or eventful strategies will not be addressed in this article.

1.2 Artists as Eventification Agents

Following Richards and Palmer (2010, pp. 33–34), cities utilize cultural events to achieve a broad range of objectives. They refer to economic, political, and social issues and are carried out by a large range of stakeholders. However, as Jakob points out, next to traditional players with their top-down policies the experience economy in terms of Joseph Pine and James H. Gilmore (1999) put forth also some new agents, such as bottom-up cultural initiatives, social associations, and other community-level actors. Among them are also artists who can be involved in planning and executing cultural events on a local level and act as important driving forces of the artist-led urban revitalization (Jakob, 2013).

As exemplified in Jakob's article "The Eventification of Place: Urban Development and Experience Consumption in Berlin and New York City," this rather new form of collaboration between different partners induces changes on different levels. On one hand, they affect the content production and the organizational framework of the events. On the other hand, they cause also changes in how artists relate to their art and presentation in public. According to Jakob, they tend to renounce the romanticized myth of the genius in favor of more practical modes of participation, often in accordance with the broader aims of the established urban growth coalition (Jakob, 2013).

This seems to be also the case with the Street Piano Project called *Play Me, I'm Yours* as designed by the British artist Luke Jerram. The concept implies that pianos, artfully painted by local artists and lettered with the invitation "Play me, I'm Yours" are placed in public spaces, waiting for potential use. Further, the artist provided a homepage on which the activities documented by strolling by individuals could be uploaded and shared in the virtual space. Commissioned first in 2008 in Birmingham, the project enjoyed great popularity and was carried out as a touring installation on a global level (Zamora, 2013).

1.2.1 The Artist and His Projects

Luke Jerram (*1974) belongs to the most popular living artists. Being trained as a sculpturer as well as a performing artist, he is working in different art fields, designing, among others, installations, and live artworks. On the first glance, the objects exhibited surprise with their formal simplicity, which, however, is not self-explanatory but serves as a stimulus for the observers to interpret and re-design them according to their own imagination.

3 STREET PIANO: AN INSTRUMENT OF URBAN CHANGE   49

To bridge the gap between single artistic practices as well as between art and science, some projects are based on scientific findings. Thus, for instance, the installation *The Museum of the Moon* is a replica of a detailed *NASA* imagery of the lunar surface. It has been presented indoors and outdoors in locations as different as the *Natural History Museum* in London and a local swimming pool. According to the artist, the installation was set up to motivate the public to contemplate on the historical, cultural, scientific, and religious aspects of the moon and its symbolism (Jerram, n.d.-c, Museum of the Moon).

A similar project is *Gaia*, which was among other venues presented also in Liverpool's *Anglican Cathedral*, attracting 200,000 visitors in just one month. In this case, a replica of Earth as seen from space by the astronauts was set up to open new observation perspectives, promote the respect for nature, and remind the visitors of the mutual social responsibility.[2] The project *In Memoriam* in turn is commemorating the victims of the COVID-19 pandemic.[3] It is comprised from flags featuring a red cross in middle of a sea of white flags. The public is invited to enter the outdoor installation and contemplate on the issue while adhering the rules of social distancing (Jerram, 2020).

1.2.2 Piano—An Instrument as an Art Object

Some features sketched can be found also in the internationally touring installation *Street Piano – Play Me, I'm Yours*, in which several pianos are put outdoors waiting for being used by anybody who wanted to do so. In general, to place a piano on a street is rather unusual: pianos are heavy and difficult to move, which makes them already as physical objects a typical indoor instrument. Also, their usage is normally restricted to closed ambientes, and consequently, they are placed in concert halls and other performance venues, bars, jazz clubs, and Honky Tonks. In the nineteenth century, pianos were predominantly located in the salons of the bourgeoisie class and associated with virtuosic pianists such as Franz Liszt or the rather helpless strumming of higher daughters, providing family entertainment (Hildebrandt, 1985).

---

[2] Another celestial body presented in the same way was Mars (Jerram, n.d.-b, Mars).

[3] Jerram explored the aesthetic dimension of viruses already before the Covid pandemic and produced for his project Glass Microbiology a glass replica of the Ebola virus (Jerram, 2011, Glass Microbiology).

Further, there is no doubt that pianos belong to the most widespread instruments of the Western hemisphere. On the one hand, they owe their popularization to the fact that the industrialization and the founding of the first piano companies, such as the British *Broadwood*, established in 1802, opened the way to mass production of the instrument. But on the other hand, they also have several musical properties which make them superior to other instruments. As pointed out by Dieter Hildebrandt, pianos are harmonic instruments with the broadest range of tones which allows the reproduction of the entire repertoire of existing music. Further, contrary to instruments such as the violin, trumpet, or horn, the sound generation is simple and avoids also with unskilled players an undesirable sound production (Hildebrandt, 1985). The instrument is applicable for any kind of music, classical or popular, and can be played by amateurs and professionals alike (Isacoff, 2012). It can be performed solo, in an ensemble or accompanied by an orchestra or used for composing, rehearsing, and music teaching.

In the nineteenth century, piano was the main source of music entertainment in private and semi-private settings. During the twentieth century, with the coming up of mass media such as record player, radio, television, and Internet, musical reception was not bound on live music anymore. Further, in popular genres such as Rock and Pop, acoustic pianos were seldom used, or they were replaced by electric ones or electronic keyboards. All this contributed to the fact that several owners were trying to dispose their useless pieces of musical furniture which allowed Jerram to acquire numerous pianos as a donation or buy them on very low costs (Jerram & Dunning, 2016).

However, this is just one part of the story, because for Luke Jerram, coming from visual arts and sculpture, a Street Piano is more than a simple music instrument. In accordance with the concept of the project, it is a kind of a "big blank canvas" (Jerram & Dunning, 2016) to be painted or decorated. For this task, amateur as well as professional volunteers with different talents, skills, and visual ideas were recruited, often connected with educational or socio-cultural institutions. Hence, the aesthetics of the paint ups ranges from simple children drawing to examples of great visual creativity, turning any single item of the mass product piano into a colorful sculpture and an individual work of art.

As different as the music played are also the designs of Street Pianos, mostly created as a teamwork. Following the premise, the more colorful the better the motifs often pick up codes of different forms of street art, such as graffiti or HipHop iconography. However, although the playable installations could be regarded also as independent objects of visual arts, for Jerram the aural and the visual component represent an inseparable unit. Hence before they get distributed to their final locations, the refurbished pianos are normally centrally exhibited on kick-off events with music: This consists of a joint performance of several pianists, staged in a circle and performing together an introduction program.

2 PRESENTATION

2.1 Data Collection and Evaluation

If the project design seems to be simple, the message behind is complex and so is its role in the festivalization and eventization of the city. To understand the polyseme dynamics of the interactive installation, an Internet-based ethnographic survey was undertaken. The method applied can be associated with research techniques such as digital ethnography (Pink et al., 2015) and Internet ethnography (Sade-Beck, 2004) though the Internet has been deployed predominantly as a data-gathering instrument as suggested by Cris Mann and Fiona Stewart (2000).

Initially the data collection were carried out in several stages between 2018 and 2021, "followed by the algorithm" as proposed by Massimo Airoldi, Davide Beraldo, and Alessandro Gandini (2016). This procedure resulted in a convolute of some 200 different items such as newspaper articles, reports, project descriptions, adverts, pictorial material, and videos. Further information, giving insights into the context, was derived from home pages, blogs, and chats.

Though the main sources of information were already existing documents, produced by different agents in their natural contexts, this methodological approach showed some problems and limitations. The database was rather fragile, and information gathered on one day might not have been found again. Following Pascal Föhr (2018), further problems comprises the fact that conventional source-critical methods cannot be applied to digital objects. The concerns affect especially the authenticity, integrity, and reliability of non-scientific material which could not be verified according to the established standards of humanities and social sciences.

This applies also to original sources such as the homepages of the artist himself and the project *Play Me, I'm Yours* (Jerram, n.d.-f, Street Pianos, About). However, though in both cases the material has been generated by Luke Jerram himself and hence being treated with corresponding constraint, it proved to be a good point of departure. Also, the supplementary materials of lesser reliability turned out to be helpful, especially videos displaying the experiential character of the project and giving inside in issues not mentioned elsewhere.

The interpretation followed the method of the hermeneutical content analysis, whereby the explanatory lens focused on the event character of the project in terms of Smith (2016) and Richards and Palmer (2010). Further in accordance with Jakob (2013), the role of the artist Luke Jerram as an agent of the urban revitalization, his cooperation with the urban growth coalition, and the takeover of his project idea by other stakeholders were of interest.

2.2   The Project Agenda

As a semi-official narrative states, the world's first Street Piano belonged to a student from Sheffield, who failed to move the heavy instrument into his flat. Hence, he left it on the street, provided a stool for it, and put up a sign inviting passers-by to sit down and play it. Despite the unstable weather in that part of the world, a lot of people followed the instruction and made music, which evoked a nation-wide attention (comp. Zamora, 2013). This episode might have served as an inspiration for the Luke Jerram's *Play Me, I'm Yours* project, though with his own words the initial spark for putting painted pianos in the urban environment came from the following observation:

> The idea for *Play Me, I'm Yours* came from visiting my local launderette. I saw the same people there each weekend and yet no one talked to one another. I suddenly realised that within a city, there must be hundreds of these invisible communities, regularly spending time with one another in silence. Placing a piano into the space was my solution to this problem, acting as a catalyst for conversation and changing the dynamics of a space. (Jerram & Dunning, 2016)

In negotiating the public space, however, for Jerram, the crucial issues were not the pianos per se, but the inscription "Play me, I'm Yours," aiming at the stimulation of the social action and addressing anybody who felt inspired. This did not apply just to the players, who could use the piano irrespective of their musical skills and abilities. Performed in a venue which is free and open to people of all backgrounds, the public also got the possibility to overcome the role of a simple listener and join the temporary (music) community by singing, dancing, or holding on to the short-lived moments of musicing in photos and videos.

Hence, according to Jerram, the importance of the actions described goes far beyond musical issues. Street music is for him a strong agent of community building as well as a vital factor of urban experience: It has the "capacity to create a sense of place" and can as such induce a "positive change within a city" (Jerram & Dunning, 2016). Therefore, as Jerram put it, the project also questions the "public ownership" over the urban space, respectively, the power relationships in the city with the intention to "provoke people into engaging, activating and claiming ownership of their urban landscape" (Jerram & Dunning, 2016). He sums up:

> I suppose my job is to ask questions about public domain, and what it is for, and who is it for, and to ask questions about how we engage with our city. I am a firm believer that this is our city, that it's owned by the people who are living in the city, and it's up to us as citizens to decide how we use it, and how we think about its transformation over the coming years. (Jerram & Dunning, 2016)

2.3 International Distribution

The first project edition was implemented in Birmingham. Its Homepage noted the following:

> In March 2008, fifteen pianos were delivered to the streets of Birmingham. Located in skate parks, industrial estates, laundrettes, precincts, bus shelters and train stations, outside pubs and football grounds, the free Street Pianos were for any member of the public to enjoy and claim ownership of. Who played them and how long they remained was up to each community. Only one was vandalised and the others were loved, played every day, personalised, and decorated. (Birmingham, 2008)

After this successful launch, the project started to tour worldwide and has been up till now installed in many cities (Table 3.1).

A comparison of selected editions shows that the core idea of the installation remains the same, irrespective of where it has been staged. However, due to local factors, the actual implementation gets a local touch. A good example is the well-documented *Play Me, I'm Yours* event as has been

54   A. BARBER-KERSOVAN

Table 3.1   The geographical distribution of the *Play Me, I'm Yours* project

Year	City
2008	Birmingham
	Sao Paulo
2009	Sydney
	Bury St Edmunds
	London
	Bristol
2010	Barcelona
	Bath
	New York
	London
	Blackburn & Burnley
	Cincinnati
	Belfast
	San Jose
	Pécs
	Grand Rapids
2011	Adelaide
	Austin
	Geneva
	London
	Tilburg
	Malta
2012	Los Angeles
	London
	Salt Lake City
	Geneva
	Paris
	Toronto
	Salem, Oregon
	Stratford, Ontario
	Toowoomba, Australia
	Perth, Australia
	Cambridge
	Hangzhou, China

(*continued*)

3 STREET PIANO: AN INSTRUMENT OF URBAN CHANGE 55

Table 3.1 (continued)

Year	*City*
2013	Monterey
	Munich
	Geneva
	Paris
	Cleveland
	Omaha
	Boston
	Santiago
2014	Shanghai, China
	Melbourne
	Mayagüez
	Mexico City
	Lima & Callao
	Luxembourg
	Grand Genève
	Albany, NY
	Paris
	Glasgow
	Stoke-on-Trent
2015	Florence, SC
	Grand Genève
	Paris
	Stockholm
	Hong Kong
	Canary Wharf
	Munich
	Canterbury
2016	Mesa, AZ
	Singapore
	Florence, SC
	Grand Genève
	Paris
	Aberdeen
	Munich
	Boston

(*continued*)

56 A. BARBER-KERSOVAN

Table 3.1 (continued)

Year	City
2017	Florence, South Carolina
	Augsburg, Germany
	Paris
	Norfolk, Virginia
	Grand Genève
	Bristol
	Munich
2018	Melbourne, Australia
	Kunitachi, Tokyo
	Arica, Chile
	Shenzhen, China
	Grand Genève, Switzerland
	The Valleys, Wales
	Munich, Germany
	Paris: Boulogne-Billancourt
2019	Shanghai, China
	Melbourne, Australia
	Augsburg, Germany
	Grand Genève, Switzerland
2020	Augsburg, Germany
	Shanghai, China
	Grand Genève, Switzerland

Own representation based on the information from the official homepage of the Street Piano Project. A global map of the project can be found under Jerram, L. (n.d.-g), Street Pianos, Global map

carried out in Melbourne in 2014.[4] It was commissioned by the *Arts Centre Melbourne*, a complex of theaters, concert halls, and other venues, mostly dedicated to the performance of high culture, but also offering some alternatives. One of them is *Betty Amsden Participation Program*, devoted to the fostering of creativity on a broad basis as well as promoting cultural democracy and the revitalization of the public space through large-scale projects (Arts Centre Melbourne, 2019).

If we believe a report by Bailey and Yang Consultants, in the project altogether, some 440,000 individuals were involved:

- 62 people who donated pianos and cash to the project
- 215 people from 31 community groups, who decorated and performed at the pianos

[4] The project has been repeated in 2018.

- 38 opening night performers
- about 2500 people who attended the free opening night event
- about 95,000 people who played the 24 pianos
- about 346,000 people who stopped to watch, take photos, and listen to the piano. (compiled from Bailey & Yang Consultants, 2014)

Further, as summed up in the evaluation, the project had the "capacity to build Melbourne's social, creative and cultural capital". The participants pointed out that the ephemeral performances gave them the feeling of "wonder", "delight," and "happiness" and praised the opportunity to "connect with strangers" and "place." As statements such as *"Play Me, I'm Yours* made the city feel more creative" and *"Play Me, I'm Yours* made the city feel more human" indicate the project changed the relationship of the public toward the city and at the same time changed the city itself. As the pianos were removed, they were painfully missed (compiled from Bailey & Yang Consultants, 2014; comp. also Arts Centre Melbourne, 2014, Video report).

Similar case was reported from Boston, where the project has been presented first in 2013 and re-installed in 2016 with 60 Street Pianos displayed (Slane, 2016). The organizer, the *Celebrity Series of Boston*, focuses predominantly on the highlight of classical music but is running also an "Arts for All" program with free community concerts, workshops, and participatory projects. For the organizer, the project "is a perfect fit for this program," explained Gary Dunning, *Celebrity Series* president, "bringing visual and performance art into the community. *Street Pianos Boston* proves art truly is everywhere and everyone can participate" (Celebrity Series of Boston, 2016). "After more than a half million Bostonians participated in Street Pianos in 2013, we knew we wanted to bring back this city-wide installation that activates public space and engages the public with the joy of live performance" (Criscitiello, 2016).

2.4   The Janus Face of Success

The growing popularity of Jerram's installations, however, turned out to be a double-edged matter, because the more they spread globally, the more frequent were the attempts of various social, cultural, or political stakeholders to copy the core ideas and use them for their own purposes. One of the most controversial appropriations was the takeover of the New York edition by *Sing for Hope*. This charity, founded in New York

58   A. BARBER-KERSOVAN

City in 2006, partners with hundreds of community-based organizations and harness to its own words "the power of the arts to create a better world" through bringing "hope, healing, and connection to millions of people in hospitals, care facilities, schools, refugee camps, transit hubs, and community spaces worldwide" (Sing for Hope, 2021).

In 2010 *Sing for Hope* realized *Play Me, I'm Yours* together with Luke Jerram but canceled further collaboration a year later. Even more, the organizer did not even tribute Jerram the authorship of his artwork and presented it as its own project under the new label *Pianos for Hope* instead. The controversy around the authorship arose from the fact that the charity claimed to have some own ideas about the implementation which were not compatible with Jerram's (NN, 2017, Sing).

Since there were also other stakeholders who appropriated the project, on one hand, *Play Me, I'm Yours* turned out to be a victim of its own success. But, on the other hand, it stimulated a mass movement of Street Pianos on a global scale. Jerram resumed:

> *Play Me, I'm Yours* has created a global movement of pianos being installed in public places across the world by organisations and individuals, for people to play. With Street Pianos popping up in towns and cities worldwide, Luke Jerram is proud that his concept for this artwork, has now become part of contemporary culture. (Jerram, n.d.-f, Street Pianos, About)

2.4.1   From Street Pianos to Piano Cities

The globally spread piano mania released a whole bundle of creative energies and stimulated the piano-centered artistic production on different levels. "Pianomen," with their grand pianos placed on self-made traveling devices, belong to the street ambience in Hamburg and Berlin. In 2018 on the *Festival of the Districts* in Vienna, a piano was daily coached from one part of the town to the other to be played (and listened to) by anybody who wanted to: A special feature was the project *Open Piano for Refugees*, providing cross-cultural exchange opportunities (DoReMi, n.d.).[5] Karen Schlimp tends to play her mobile piano while three mates of her drive it on a specially fitted bicycle (Schlimp, n.d.). Another example is Joe Löhrmann who combined his two passions, music and traveling,

---

[5] Similar to Play Me, I'm Yours, this project also found offshoots in different cities and expended to other countries.

into a *Traveling Piano* project, giving in tourist hotspots concerts under the blue sky (Löhrmann, n.d.).

Further, *Play Me, I'm Yours* events and its derivates have been from the beginning accompanied by workshops, concerts, and related activities, or they enlarged already existing musical events. A good example is the *LeedsPianoTrail2021* project that accompanied the traditional *20th Leeds International Piano Competition* (Leeds International, 2021a, b). The project was developed in partnership with *LeedsBID* (Leeds Business Improvement District), an independent, but business-led organization whose mission is to "improve Leeds City Centre for all" and "to animate the city centre to stimulate the local business" (LeedsBid, n.d.).

The two-week lasting event featured a unique series of installations made entirely from up-cycled pianos created by the Edinburgh-based *Pianodrome*[6] collective, alongside 10 instruments which have been transformed by professional artists and community groups into playable works of art. The project itself, consisting of some **450** different events, was carried out by several socially engaged stakeholders covering a broad spectrum from artist communities involved in urban placemaking till initiatives concerned with wellbeing, sustainability, and women issues. Bringing music to the whole city, the project aimed at the encouragement of the public to explore its urban environment (Leeds International Piano Competition 2021, 2021b, Piano Trail).

Similar forms of experiencing the city by searching for Street Pianos were realized also in other municipalities. In some cases, such as, for instance, in Boston, there was/is even a tendency to put up at least one piano in a borough/quarter (Criscitiello, 2016) to create an invisible net of urban connections with Street Pianos as points of reference. Further, guided tours to remote piano locations, mostly on foot or on bicycles, are organized and piano maps printed to help participants to find (and play) as many pianos as possible.

In some cases, individual piano events were merged into city-wide spectacles that ran under the trademark "Piano Cities." Among the first was *Piano City Milan* which started in 2011 with a 30-pianist marathon foreshowing the event. Also, the consequent editions, though predominantly concentrating on what was called "quality culture" music, brought several musical innovations, such as a symphony for 21 pianos by Daniele

---

[6] Pianodrome is a unique venue the interieur of which has been made of parts of de-constructed pianos.

60   A. BARBER-KERSOVAN

Lombardi, which opened the 2013 festival: as the stage served *Rotonda della Besana*, a former graveyard for the poor. In 2016, 50 uninterrupted hours of piano music were presented, and the festival increased its presence in the outskirts. It also grows significantly every year to embrace unexpected spaces and venues and even teamed with the *Expo 2015* (Piano City Milano, n.d.).

Aspiring to be engaging, participative, and open for everyone, the program is realized by a collaboration of many cultural and institutional partners and encompasses concerts, piano lessons, workshops, tributes to great musicians and other piano events. Further, even more explicitly as in other examples given so far, *Piano City Milan* presents itself as "the soundtrack of the city: inspiration and tool for its regeneration", which "evolved alongside the metamorphosis and rebirth of Milan" (Piano City Milano, n.d.).

Also, this project had several copycats, such as, for instance, the project *Piano City Berlin*, which, however, is predominantly known for the revival of the so-called Hausmusik (Mertens, 2010). Further Piano City projects were carried out in Naples, Novi Sad, Trieste, Palermo, and New York (Piano City Berlin, 2019). In the pandemic year 2020, the three days of piano concerts were streamed live under the hashtag "The soundtrack of your city" with pianists from different countries performing from their home music from different genres (Piano City Milano, n.d.).

3   INTERPRETATION

A content analysis of the self-presentations of the projects discussed reveals that to a certain extent, all of them follow a similar basic narrative. This narrative implies that Street Pianos projects transcend the boundaries of a purely aesthetically conceived music performance and are loaded with social and political meanings. Thus, driven by hedonism and consumerism, on one hand, piano musicing might provide fun, play, or self-realization and satisfy the need for participation. On the other hand, however, following the notions of the experience economy in terms of Joseph Pine and James H. Gilmore (1999), these projects can be seen also as serving the municipal policy by contributing to the animation of the urban atmosphere, revitalization of neglected parts of the towns, and strengthening the urban identity.

To understand the mechanisms that make pianos an *Instrument of Change*, as the documentary film about Luke Jerram's *Play Me, I'm Yours* installations has been titled,[7] the interpretation of the phenomenon will be embedded in the larger context of the eventization of cities. This "eventful turn" in terms of Andrea Pavoni (2017) and Richards and Palmer (2010) is characterized by a diversity of approaches and (policy) aims that makes it impossible to bring them down to a single enumerator. The same applies also for the interpretation of the Street Piano projects. Though they show several similar traits, not all of them apply to all examples and they are also not evident in all cases respectively in the same form. Therefore, as pars pro toto the focus will be directed toward Luke Jerram's project with the following points proposed for further consideration:

- By being put into the public space a Street Piano loses the image of an elitist instrument, and the inscription "Play Me, I'm Yours" invites everybody to use it irrespectively of his or her musical skills and abilities. The ephemeral performances are addressed at the players and listeners likewise and serve broader social purposes in terms of "culture for all". Further, as a rule, after being used for some two or three weeks, the instruments are donated to local schools or other social institutions. In this respect, the project shows the traits of those forms of eventification, which are according to Jakob (2013) and Richards and Palmer (2010, p. 365) primarily socially oriented and can make a sustainable contribution to wellbeing, education, and community building beyond the duration of the actual installation.
- The notion that the Street Piano projects are "culture for all" is being strengthened by the fact that they are performed in a venue summarized under the term "the street." According to Vikas Mehta, "the street" is a "quintessential social public space" (Mehta, 2013, p. 3) with several cultural, economic, social, legal, and political implications. Free of charge and open to people of all backgrounds (Smith, 2016, p. 35) is the street the most heterogeneous space of a society, super-positioning different needs, actions and functions and mirroring the diversity of the urban population. Further, streets provide also "settings for sociability" (Mehta 2013, p. 3) and act with Andrew Smith (2016) and Paul Simson (2011) as performance venues, whereby some cultural forms such as street music or street art explicitly refer to this issue.

---

[7]This documentary, directed by Maureen Ni Fiann and co-directed by Tom Rochester, was award winning and presented in 2017 among others at the New Urbanism, now Better Cities Film Festival (We are Moving Stories, 2017).

Artistic activities in public spaces have a long tradition of official events as well as (mostly undesirable) spontaneous interventions in the urban fabric (Smith, 2016, pp. 21ff). During the last decades, however, "the street" has been rediscovered as a stage for several performative practices, providing a welcome contribution to the so-called urban atmosphere. The program of the New York metro called *Music Under New York* (Tanenbaum, 1997) is as representative for this trend as is the busking culture in London which has been put under the direct patronage of the Mayors Boris Johnson and Sadiq Kahn in order "to make London the busking capital of the world" (BBC, n.d.).

In this respect is the Street Piano project in line with a broader trend to use the street as a performance venue. As already elaborated by Richards and Palmer (2010, p. 27) and further developed by Andrew Smith (2016, p. 18), events are more frequently staged outside locations specially designed for musical or sportive purposes. They are performed in public spaces and regarded as valuable tools to animate the urban atmosphere. This narrative is echoed in the statements by Luke Jerram and manifests itself also in other Street Piano projects, especially in the goal setting of the *Piano City Milan* festival.

- A further important issue is the fact that Street Pianos are distributed across town so that the whole city is acting at the same time as a dislocated outdoor gallery and a city-wide music venue. Also, this aspect is not specific for the Street Piano projects only. According to Andrew Smith (2016, p. 196), during the last decades the distinction between event venues and urban public spaces has been increasingly blurred, and the functioning of public spaces as well as their management and regulation increasingly resembles those of venues. Similarly, Richards and Palmer (2010, p. 27) also argue stating that in the process of eventization, the "entire city becomes a stage across which a succession of events is paraded". Moreover, according to Andrew Smith during the performative transformation of street spaces into performance places, a double way of staging can be observed: As the city acts as a stage, the events also stage the city in a particular way (Smith, 2016, p. 2).
- As Regina Bittner reports in her publication about the construction of urban experience spaces, the city became a *mise-en-scene* for the staged urbanity (Bittner, 2002). Public space is experienced as a place of fun and adventure, whereby the self-structuring of social

processes is mostly mediated through digital technology. With Hanno Rauterberg reasons for this experiential turn should be sought for in the hyper-individualism of the digital modernity, which induced a new community spirit, the longing for collective experiences, and the desire for delight and pleasure (Rauterberg, 2013).

Also, the ephemeral Street Piano interventions correspond with the postmodern singularization, differentiation, and individualization of lifestyles and the increased demand for symbolic goods as described by Gerhard Schulze (2005) in his concept of an adventure society. However, following the theoretical explanations by Smith (2016) and Richards and Palmer (2010), the experience oriented eventization of culture is not pure entertainment, but a constitutive element of the current municipal policy of leisure. In relation to the subject dealt with here, this aspect was articulated particularly vividly in the case of the *Piano City Milan* project.

- The organization of city-wide events requires a close cooperation between many different partners, such as political bodies, cultural organizations, promoters, businesses, and voluntary associations (Richards & Palmer, 2010, p. 305). Doreen Jakob remarks that under this conditions, eventification can generate new ways of integrating different stakeholders into the urban growth coalitions (Jakob, 2013), which might include also grassroots initiatives.

This applies also to Jerram's *Play Me, I'm Yours* project. The 2008 edition was commissioned by the festival organization *Fierce* from Birmingham, which started off in 1998 as *Queerfest*. For the topic discussed is of importance that *Fierce* understands itself as a "relevant, fresh, and feisty voice for the city" and "has been where the incredible happens [...], populating theatres, galleries and hidden, unusual, or out-of-the-ordinary spaces" (Fierce, n.d.). The animation of the city was also the topic of another artwork Jerram carried out in cooperation with *Fierce* called *Sky Orchestra*: In this project, cities were sonicated with "music for sleeping people" broadcast from several floating air balloons. Also, this project was understood as a form of "provocative urban art" questioning the "boundaries of public artwork, private space and the ownership of the sky" (Jerram, n.d.-e, Sky Orchestra).

64   A. BARBER-KERSOVAN

However, it must be pointed out that despite its political rhetoric *Fierce* is by no means oppositional underground, but an *Arts Council England National Portfolio Organisation*, relying on public funds. In the same sense also Jerram's Do-it-yourself project is less spontaneous as it might seem, but carefully planned and carried out with the help of local partners such as the *Celebrity Series* from Boston, the *Arts Centre Melbourne*, or the charity *Sing for Hope*, which organized the first Jerram's project in New York. Jerram and his organizational team provide just tool kits for implementation, give advice and guidance, set up the city website, and visit each city to help with the installation (Jerram & Dunning, 2016). The main bulk of the work, however, is done by local partners, who have the local knowledge required to select locations for the pianos, get permits, find local artists and community groups to decorate the pianos, as well as to raise the necessary funds (ibid.).

- Furthermore, it stands out that Jerram's street project has been commissioned by several established organizations and presented in the framework of prominent festivals. Among the partners worth mentioning are the *British Council*, the Mayor of London, the *United Nations*, the *Royal Shakespeare Company*, and several other prominent organizers. Also, occasions on which Jerram's projects were presented belong to the most prestigious events of the time such as *London 2012 Olympics, Pan Am Games, Commonwealth Games*, and the *European Capital of Culture 2010* (Jerram, n.d.-f, Street Pianos, About).

As locations, eminent art center and galleries such as *Metropolitan Museum of Art* must be referenced. Further, Jerram's work was also presented on festivals such as the *London Festival* and the *Glastonbury Festival of Contemporary Arts*. Worth mentioning are also collaborations with different scientific organizations such as the *UK Space Agency, The Natural Environment Research Council, The Science Museum London*, and several science and cultural departments from British and foreign universities (Jerram, n.d.-d, Partnerships).

The collaboration with numerous institutions and organizations from many different fields allows staging of Jerram's touring artworks on a global scale, so that the micro dynamics of single performative acts sum up in impressive numbers, other artists can just dream of. Thus, for instance, the artwork *Museum of the Moon* was supposedly installed more than 150 times in 30 different countries and experienced by more than 10 million people. When presented in the *National History Museum*, 2.1 million people visited the show making it one of the most popular exhibitions in its history (Jerram, n.d.-c, Museum of the Moon).

The *Play Me I'm Yours* project can also boast with impressive numbers. It was first commissioned in Birmingham, UK, in 2008 with 15 pianos located across the city. The project lasted three weeks, and according to the organizers during that time some 14,000 people played the pianos or listened to the performances. If we believe Jerram's homepage up till April 2020 as despite the pandemic, the project was presented in Augsburg, Shanghai, and Genève where some 2000 pianos have been installed in over 60 cities with an estimated reach of 20 million people (Jerram, n.d.-f, Street Pianos, About).

- As Doreen Jakob (2013, p. 447) reports, eventification also fosters a new relationship between the urban growth coalition and the individual artists. Andrea Pavoni noticed in this connection that in the current eventification processes, some aesthetical practices "increasingly migrate from the realm of artistic avant-gardes and activism into the toolbox of neoliberal ideology" (Pavoni, 2017, n.p.). However, based on the examples Jakob studied, artists activities are not necessarily taken over by politics and economically stronger groups but rather designed to attract these interests (Jakob, 2013, p. 451).

If that might have been the case also with Jerram's *Play Me, I'm Yours* project, it could not be determined from the material available. But as can be concluded from his statements, he understood music as an important place maker and as such capable to influence the urban environment. Further Jerram repeatedly pointed out that he is not only encouraging the passers-by to express themselves and communicate with each other. He understands himself also as a critical interrogator of the use of the urban space he identifies as "cold" (BBC News Channel, 2009) and takes up the role of a campaigner reclaiming the ownership of the urban landscape in the name of the public.

66   A. BARBER-KERSOVAN

- Since according to Andrea Pavoni in the framework of the neoliberal urbanization also individuals and small organisation can convey messages and pursue socio-cultural objectives (Pavoni, 2017), also Jerram's grassroots understanding of urbanity could be put in line with the aims of the urban municipal policies. Jacob however remarked that the "down-scaling" of festivalization to local issues and individual creators has been accompanied with the "up-scaling" of artists' entrepreneurial activities and their adaptation to the economic strategies of the growth coalition (Jakob, 2013, p. 451).

These tendencies can also be identified in the manner Jerram presents himself in the public. He and his team are skilled cultural promoters, with several projects simultaneously touring on a global scale. Their launch is—as it was the case in New York, Augsburg, or Munich—often undertaken by the city Mayors and accompanied with extensive media coverage. The survey of the press material neatly displayed on Jerram's homepage, however, reveals that most articles are reprints of press information provided by the artist.

- Further, it should not remain unmentioned that the operational basis of Jerram's activities is the *Luke Jerram Ltd* with the company number 06775974. It has been incorporated in December 2008 to support his artistic creation (Gov. UK, 2021) and currently employs four people with Jerram as a Director. The company organizes the running installations but is also taking commissions from different stakeholders to develop new projects according to their ideas (Jerram, n.d.-d, Partnerships).
- Finally, Jerram's project should be embedded into the global framework of eventification as a tool of municipal policies. Due to the neoliberal "enforcement of the market as a general organizational principle of the society" cities must face the "competitive pressure of the global economy" (Mattissek, 2008, p. 14). However, striving to highlight their competitive advantages, they often take over models and event formats that already proved to be successful elsewhere (Richards & Palmer, 2010, p. 53). They also tend to advertise the uniqueness of the respective location by using the same verbal and iconographic stereotypes, which leads to the "competitive standardization" of the communicated cityscapes (Mattissek, 2008, p. 17) and the harmonization of consumption patterns and live styles.

Similar applies to the project *Play Me, I'm Yours* by Luke Jerram, whose Street Piano events are reproduced and simultaneously staged in several cities at the same time. Though the singular projects follow to a certain extent the intrinsic logic of cities in terms of Helmut Berking und Martina Löw (2008) by adjusting to local circumstances, the core of the projects stays worldwide the same. Even more: The touring installations do not claim the authenticity of the original but work with replicas which are multiplied and installed in different urban and cultural settings. Also, homepages of singular cities which have their own *Play Me, I'm Yours* websites with photos, videos, and stories about the Street Pianos are structured in the same way conveying the same message.

Hence the project might present itself as "street music" with connotations such as "genuine," "sincere," "honest," "real," and "authentic," playing with democratic allusions on the "culture for all" and "reclaiming the ownership of the urban landscape." There is also no doubt that for those involved performative moments of piano musicing have a high experience value, providing short moments of creativity, joy, and happiness. Also, the contribution of the project to social engagement, education, and community building should not be disregarded (comp. also Jakob, 2013, p. 455). However, the features described must be counter weighted by the fact that it is a prefabricated model that is reproduced *en masse*, providing interchangeable variations of sameness on a global scale and as such paradoxically diminishing the transformative power of an *Instrument of Change*.

REFERENCES

Airoldi, M., Beraldo, D., & Gandini, A. (2016). Follow the algorithm: An exploratory investigation of music on YouTube. *Poetics, 57*, 1–13. https://doi.org/10.1016/j.poetic.2016.05.001

Arts Centre Melbourne. (2014). *Video report by Bailey and Yung Consultants.* Retrieved March 23, 2021, from https://www.youtube.com/watch?v=rHvTmRcT4_8&list=PLR93WjsE3izJu_-vKIkhWP_fZNehgNTIV&index=5

Arts Centre Melbourne. (2019). *Public realm program.* Retrieved March 21, 2021, from https://www.artscentremelbourne.com.au/join-support/donate/public-realm-program

Bailey & Yang Consultants. (2014). *Play Me, I'm Yours Evaluation report.* A report written for Arts Centre Melbourne by Bailey and Yang Consultants about the impact of the Play Me, I'm Yours project on participants, donors and the general public. Retrieved February 12, 2021, from https://de.scribd.com/document/351077743/Play-Me-I-m-Yours-Evaluation-FULL-REPORT

68   A. BARBER-KERSOVAN

Barber-Kersovan, A. (2007). Creative class, creative industries, creative city. Ein musikpolitisches Paradigma. In D. Helms & T. Phleps (Eds.), *Sound and the city. Populäre Musik im urbanen Kontext* (pp. 11–30). transcript.

Barber-Kersovan, A. (2021). Musikalische Neubauten des 21. Jahrhunderts: Kulturelle, ökonomische und symbolische Dimensionen der musikbezogenen Starchitecture. *Muzikoloski zbornik/Musicological Annual, 57*(1), 201–227.

BBC (British Broadcasting Corporation). (n.d.). *Let's busk it.* [Blog]. Retrieved April 2, 2021, from https://www.bbc.co.uk/programmes/articles/Ll6QRXBFvF8bJDrGCfMT4g/lets-busk-it

BBC News Channel. (2009). *Art project puts pianos on street.* Retrieved March 17, 2021, from http://news.bbc.co.uk/2/hi/uk_news/england/london/8114859.stm

Berking, H., & Löw, M. (Eds.). (2008). *Die Eigenlogik der Städte. Neue Wege der Stadtforschung.* Campus.

Betz, G., Hitzler, R., & Pfadenhauer, M. (2011). Zur Einleitung: Eventisierung des Urbanen. In G. Betz, R. Hitzler, & M. Pfadenhauer (Eds.), *Urbane Events.* VS Verlag für Sozialwissenschaften.

Birmingham 2008. (2008). *Home.* Retrieved August 21, 2021, from http://streetpianos.com/birmingham2008/

Bittner, R. (Ed.). (2002). *Die Stadt als Event. Zur Konstruktion urbaner Erlebnisräume.* Campus-Verlag.

Celebrity Series of Boston. (2016). *Street Pianos Boston 2016, Play Me, I'm Yours.* Retrieved June 23, 2021, from https://www.celebrityseries.org/live-performances/public-performance-projects/street-pianos-boston-2016/

Criscitiello, A. (2016). *Celebrity series announces locations for Street Pianos Boston, Broadway World Music.* Retrieved June 27, 2021, from https://www.broadwayworld.com/bwwmusic/article/Celebrity-Series-Announces-Locations-for-Street-Pianos-Boston-20160907

DoReMi. (n.d.). *Open piano for refugees.* [Homepage]. Retrieved April 4, 2021, from https://openpianoforrefugees.com/doremi/

Fierce. (n.d.). *About.* [Homepage]. Retrieved May 30, 2021, from https://wearefierce.org/about/

Florida, R. (2002). *The rise of the creative class: And how it's transforming work, leisure, community, and everyday life.* Basic Books.

Föhr, P. (2018). *Historische Quellenkritik im Digitalen Zeitalter.* Universität Basel. Retrieved June 2, 2021, from https://edoc.unibas.ch/64111/1/F%C3%B6hr_Pascal-Historische_Quellenkritik_im_Digitalen_Zeitalter-2018.pdf

Gov. UK. (2021). *Luke Jerram Limited.* Retrieved June 29, 2021, from https://find-and-update.company-information.service.gov.uk/company/06775974/filing-history

Häußermann, H., & Siebel, W. (1993). *Festivalisierung der Stadtpolitik.* Springer (Leviathan 13).

3 STREET PIANO: AN INSTRUMENT OF URBAN CHANGE   69

Hildebrandt, D. (1985). *Pianoforte oder der Roman des Klaviers im 19. Jahrhundert.* dtv Verlagsgesellschaft.

Hitzler, R. (2011). *Eventisierung: Drei Fallstudien zum marketingstrategischen Massenspaß.* VS Verlag für Sozialwissenschaften / Springer Fachmedien.

Isacoff, S. (2012). *A natural history of the piano: The instrument, the music, the musicians – From Mozart to modern Jazz and everything in between.* Knopf Doubleday Publishing.

Jakob, D. (2013). The eventification of place: Urban development and experience consumption in Berlin and New York City. *European Urban and Regional Studies, 20*(4), 447–459.

Jerram, L. (2011). *Glass microbiology. Meet the artist: Luke Jerram. Corning Museum of Glass.* [Video]. Retrieved February 13, 2021, from https://www.youtube.com/watch?v=UjU0lzM1LTw

Jerram, L. (2020). *In memoriam – Artwork by Luke Jerram.* [Video]. Retrieved March 23, 2021, from https://www.youtube.com/watch?v=DwmGGKo-Hqo

Jerram, L. (n.d.-a). *Luke Jerram.* [Homepage]. Retrieved March 23, 2021, from https://www.lukejerram.com/

Jerram, L. (n.d.-b). *Mars.* [Homepage]. Retrieved March 23, 2021, from https://my-mars.org/about/

Jerram, L. (n.d.-c). *Museum of the Moon.* [Homepage]. Retrieved March 30, 2021, from https://my-moon.org/about/

Jerram, L. (n.d.-d). *Partnerships.* [Homepage]. Retrieved April 12, 2021, from https://www.lukejerram.com/partnerships/

Jerram, L. (n.d.-e). *Sky Orchestra.* [Homepage]. Retrieved February 17, 2021, from http://www.skyorchestra.co.uk/

Jerram, L. (n.d.-f). Street Pianos. About. [Homepage]. Retrieved April 2, 2021, from http://www.streetpianos.com/about/

Jerram, L. (n.d.-g). *Street Pianos.* Global map [Homepage]. Retrieved July 3, 2021, from http://www.streetpianos.com/map/

Jerram, L., & Dunning, G. (2016, November 10). The inspiration of Play Me, I'm Yours Street Pianos. With Founder, Luke Jerram. *Artist Waves.* Retrieved February 17, 2021, from https://medium.com/@ArtistWaves/the-inspiration-of-play-me-im-yours-street-pianos-with-founder-luke-jarram-6eb182b9f094

Landry, C. (2008). *The creative city: A toolkit for urban innovators.* Routledge.

Leeds International Piano Competition 2021. (2021a). *About.* [Homepage]. Retrieved June 25, 2021, from https://www.leedspiano.com/about-the-leeds/

Leeds International Piano Competition 2021. (2021b). *Piano trail.* [Homepage]. Retrieved March 29, 2012, from https://www.leedspiano.com/piano-trail-2021/

LeedsBid. (n.d.). *About us.* [Homepage]. Retrieved July 23, 2021, from https://www.leedsbid.co.uk/about-us/

70   A. BARBER-KERSOVAN

Löhrmann, J. (n.d.). *Traveling Piano*. [Homepage]. Retrieved March 11, 2021, from https://www.mytravelingpiano.com

Mann, C., & Stewart, F. (2000). *Internet communication and qualitative research – A handbook for researching online*. SAGE.

Mattissek, A. (2008). *Die neoliberale Stadt. Diskursive Repräsentationen im Stadtmarketing deutscher Großstädte*. transcript.

Mehta, V. (2013). *The street: A quintessential social public space*. Routledge.

Mertens, D. (2010, October 13). *Festival Piano City – Hausmusik für Fremde*. Der Tagesspiegel. Retrieved April 12, 2021, from https://www.tagesspiegel.de/berlin/stadtleben/festival-piano-city-hausmusik-fuer-fremde/1955594.html

NN. (2017). *Sing For hope (2017): Pop-up Pianos' comes to NYC streets next week, without creator Luke Jerram*. Retrieved July 5, 2021, from https://www.huffpost.com/entry/sing-for-hopes-pianos_n_872575

Pavoni, A. (2017). Art Time City on the temporality of urban interventions. *Cidades* [Online], 34. Retrieved March 23, 2021, from http://journals.openedition.org/cidades/409

Piano City Berlin. (2019). [Homepage]. Retrieved February 12, 2021, from http://pianocity-berlin.com/

Piano City Milano. (n.d.). *The soundtrack of your city*. [Homepage]. Retrieved January 26, 2021, from https://www.pianocitymilano.it/associazione?lang=en

Pine, J., & Gilmore, J. (1999). *The Experience Economy*. Harvard Business School Press.

Pink, S., Horst, H., Postal, J., Hjorth, L., Lewis, T., & Tacchi, J. (2015). *Digital ethnography. Principles and practices*. Sage Publications.

Rauterberg, H. (2013). *Wir sind die Stadt. Urbanes Leben in der Digitalmoderne*. Suhrkamp.

Richards, G., & Palmer, R. (2010). *Eventful cities: Cultural management and urban revitalisation*. Elsevier.

Sade-Beck, L. (2004, June 1). *Internet ethnography online and offline*. Retrieved May 2, 2021, from https://journals.sagepub.com/doi/full/10.1177/160940690400300204

Schlimp, K. (n.d.). *Pianomobil. Kunst im öffentlichen Raum*. [Homepage]. Retrieved February 7, 2021, from https://pianomobile.com/performances/pianomobile/

Schulze, G. (2005). *Die Erlebnisgesellschaft: Kultursoziologie der Gegenwart*. Campus.

Simson, P. (2011). Street performance and the city public space, sociality, and intervening in the everyday. *Space and Culture, 14*(4), 415–430. https://doi.org/10.1177/1206331211412270

Sing for Hope. (2021). *Creating a better world through the arts*. Retrieved May 29, 2021, from https://singforhope.org/who-we-are/

Slane, Kevin. (2016). *Here's where you can play all 60 of the Boston Street Pianos. The return of the public art and music display is music to the city's ears.* Retrieved May 29, 2021, from https://www.boston.com/culture/music/2016/09/22/heres-where-you-can-play-all-60-of-the-boston-street-pianos/

Smith, A. (2016). *Events in the city. Using public spaces as event venues.* Routledge.

Tanenbaum, S. (1997). *Underground harmonies: Music and politics in the subways of New York.* Taylor & Francis Ltd.

We Are Moving Stories. (2017). *New urbanism film festival – Instrument of change: Street Piano.* Retrieved March 24, 2021, from http://www.wearemovingstories.com/we-are-moving-stories-films/2017/10/23/new-urbanism-film-festival-instrument-of-change-street-piano

Zamora, C. (2013, May 29; updated December 6, 2017). City songs: A brief history of the Street Piano. *Huffpost.* Retrieved December 28, 2020, from https://www.huffpost.com/entry/street-pianos_b_3351959

CHAPTER 4

Tango Music: Between Heritage and Transnational Resources. The Geographies of Tango In or From Buenos Aires

Elsa Broclain, Francesca Cominelli, Sébastien Jacquot, and Élodie Salin

Abstract Listed in 2009 as part of UNESCO's Representative List of the Intangible Cultural Heritage of Humanity by Uruguay and Argentina, tango is defined as "a genre that originally involved dance, music, poetry and singing". However, tango music today appears more as the backdrop

---

E. Broclain
Paris, France
e-mail: Elsa.broclain@gmail.com

F. Cominelli • S. Jacquot (✉)
IREST – EIREST, University Paris 1 Panthéon-Sorbonne, Paris, France
e-mail: Francesca.Cominelli@univ-paris1.fr; sebastien.jacquot@univ-paris1.fr

É. Salin
Laboratoire Espaces et Sociétés, Le Mans Université, Le Mans, France
e-mail: elodie.salin@univ-lemans.fr

© The Author(s), under exclusive license to Springer Nature
Singapore Pte Ltd. 2024
S. Guillard et al. (eds.), *New Geographies of Music 2*, Geographies of
Media, https://Doi.org/10.1007/978-981-97-2072-9_4

73

74   E. BROCLAIN ET AL.

to a practice that is essentially expressed through dance, from milonga venues to the World Tango Festival or tourist tango shows. Our contribution thus questions the place of tango music in contrast to dance from the dual perspective of its geographies and its transformations, in connection with public policies for the development, recognition and preservation of this practice. The focus on dance and the stabilisation of the dance repertoire on the music of the Golden Age of tango, from the middle of the twentieth century, has marginalised live music. However, heritage policies with respect to tango music in Buenos Aires and Montevideo focus on musicians and their achievements through commemorative practices, museum collections or the establishment of institutions to ensure intergenerational transmission. The musicians themselves navigate between different musical scenes, with tourists or more specialised audiences, learn to dance to meet the expectations of practitioners and at the same time hybridise tango with other music genres. Musical choices and mobility strategies then make it possible to identify the trajectories and careers of the musicians within the worlds of tango marked by the pre-eminence of dance. This chapter is based on collective investigations carried out between 2016 and 2020 in several places (Buenos Aires, Montevideo, Paris and France) in order to better understand the effects of the mobility of tourists and practitioners on the heritage creation, development and recognition of tango.

Keywords Tango • Intangible heritage • Movements • Music • Buenos Aires • Montevideo

1   INTRODUCTION

Inscribed in 2009 on the Representative List of the Intangible Cultural Heritage (ICH) of Humanity, tango encompasses multiple practices between poetry, dance and music that build, embody and express a certain relationship with the city, in Buenos Aires (Argentina) and, to a lesser extent, in Montevideo (Uruguay). The lyrics and notes of tango refer to the urban space, developing a geographical imaginary in music songs, and shape a memory of the city and its inhabitants in a nostalgic way. However, in contemporary performances, the music appears more as a backdrop to a practice of tango that is essentially expressed through dance. Indeed, dance is the central reason why practitioners from all over the world come to Buenos Aires, supported by a whole network of actors from the economies of intimacy (Törnqvist, 2013), and a sharp contrast can be noted between the number of milongas (venues dedicated to tango dance) in the city and the possibilities of listening to live music. This contemporary pre-eminence of dance is accentuated by the tourism development of tango, including shows at the Mundial de Tango (world tango dance tournament). In contrast, the heritage creation approach gives more importance to the music (Apprill, 2016), both in Buenos Aires and Montevideo, within museum collections or through the various monuments marking the history and tradition of tango in the city (monument to the bandoneon, statues of and plaques commemorating various composers and musicians). The music seems to be experienced preferentially as an indication of the glorious past of tango.

What then are the geographies and forms of manifestation of tango music, and more generally within tango practices? This question can be answered in two ways. First, what are the effects of the heritage creation and tourism development of tango on musical practices and on the dissociation between music and dance? Finally, how do musicians take their place within the worlds of tango, and what geographical and artistic strategies do they adopt?

This issue echoes the works of authors that have analysed the links between geography and music, with works exploring the relations between fixity and mobility (Connell & Gibson, 2002), from the point of view of the production of identities (Machin-Autenrieth, 2015), or the impacts of music on territories and the transformation of places (Canova, 2013), and the effects of the mobilities of musicians, music, tourists (Gibson & Connell, 2005). Finally, we take into account the way in which music also becomes heritage, due to the growing interest of cultural industries and local authorities in creating a link between music and place, and making it a factor of local identities and a driver of new economic activities (Cohen et al., 2015). However, the process of tourism development and heritage making also raises the question of their impacts on musical practice (Lashua et al., 2014). The notion of scene and their variations (Peterson & Bennett, 2004) allows us to study these transformations. We can consider tango as belonging to several scenes that are centred on Buenos Aires, the capital of tango, but also connected at a global level, through festivals, mobility of musicians and tango practitioners, constituting a translocal scene. However, if the notion of scene encompasses all the practices associated with music (places, listening practices, dance, etc.) (Peterson & Bennett, 2004), differentiated tango scenes coexist in the same places, dominated by the pre-eminence of the practice of dance, especially for tourists, of which music is just an adjuvant.

Our contribution questions the place of tango music from the dual perspective of its geographies and its transformations, in connection with public policies aimed at the development, recognition and preservation of this practice. We consider the geographies of tango music in its relation to the two emblematic cities where it emerged and is practiced (Buenos Aires and Montevideo), but also at other scales due to the international movements of musicians and the globalisation of tango. This multi-sited approach is crucial to unveil the opposition between mobility and fixity in the practice and promotion of tango music at several scales and in various places.

First, we will examine the place of music and musicians in the way tango is experienced and promoted, focusing on Buenos Aires, usually described as the capital of tango. Then in the third section, we will look at the policies towards tango music in Buenos Aires and Montevideo from the point of view of its heritage creation and its development and transmission. This comparison will highlight the different roles music can play in the framework of the policies of valorisation of tango: supporting dance-based marketing policies in Buenos Aires, or as a strategy of singularisation through music in Montevideo. Finally, in the fourth section of the paper, we will shift our perspective from places to musicians, analyzing how musicians position themselves as actors of tango, both on the stages of the Río de la Plata basin and through increasingly transnational movements (Paris and France will then be used to identify these mobilities and their logics). Musical choices and mobility strategies will then make it possible to identify the trajectories and careers of the musicians within the worlds of tango marked by the pre-eminence of dance.

This chapter is based on a collective investigation carried out between 2016 and 2020 in order to better understand the effects of the mobility of tourists and practitioners on the heritage creation, development and recognition of tango. This research has been conducted in three main locations: Buenos Aires, Montevideo, Paris (and France). It is multi-sited, and this allowed us to understand the globalisation of tango and the role that its music occupies, from the study of its central and more peripheral places. Buenos Aires is the capital of tango, and the main tango destination, concentrating tango events, musicians, practitioners. Montevideo is also a place of birth of tango, but less renowned, concentrating less practitioners, musicians, tourists, and offering a different relationship to tango music. The research conducted in France allows us to question the mobilities and diffusions of tango, from the perspective of a dynamic periphery. We conducted 104 interviews with tourists and practitioners in these different locations, including DJs, musicians, organisers of milongas, festival organisers, music and dance teachers, choreographers and dancers. A part of the investigations in France has been carried out in the context of a research project, funded by the French Ministry of Culture and directed by Francisco Leiva, which aimed at producing the files linked to the inclusion of tango in the inventory of the intangible cultural heritage of France, and involved 19 organisers of milongas and 16 organisers of tango festivals. In addition, we conducted an observation of different tango venues as well as an analysis of available documentation (festival posters and programmes, tourist guides, museography of tango museums).

2 A MUSIC AT THE SERVICE OF THE PRACTICE OF DANCE?

2.1 From Nostalgia to Remobilisation

During the twentieth century, tango marked the city of Buenos Aires as one of its main identifiers, its soundtrack and its memory. Even today, tango still permeates the soundscape of the city: around the milongas, when turning on the radio and in the tourist areas of certain districts strongly associated with it (La Boca and San Telmo). Tango can be heard playing in souvenir shops, in shows for tourists, or performed by musicians in public space. Although tango is no longer the main music heard in the city, as it was the case during its "Golden Age" (between 1935 and 1955), it is the music genre that is immediately associated with the metropolis. This identification between Buenos Aires and tango dates back a long time and is concomitant with the spread of tango to other continents in the first quarter of the twentieth century.

At that time, several dozen Argentinian musicians settled in Paris and recounted their homesickness in certain tangos, following the example of poet Enrique Cadícamo:

Lejano Buenos Aires ¡qué lindo que has de estar!
Ya van para diez años que me viste zarpar...
Aquí, en este Montmartre, fobourg sentimental,

78 E. BROCLAIN ET AL.

> *yo siento que el recuerdo me clava su puñal.*[1]
> *Anclao en París (1931)*

Tango sings regret for a Buenos Aires that is faraway or transformed by urban development, and nourishes a spatial identity for the city. Depicted as a childhood district, a dominant metaphorical space in the geography of tango, the city is imbued with the ideal of an urban culture of social mixing. This nostalgic view of places shapes the city and its representations, and permeates the lives of city dwellers (Gervais-Lambony, 2012).

However, while the tango culture persists in the urban imagination, its importance has greatly diminished. It notably entered a phase of decline in the 1960s in Argentina and globally, due in particular to an increasing role of other music genres and an internal aesthetic crisis. From the mid-1950s onwards, the Argentinian music industry opened up to new genres (rock, folk) aimed at younger generations and rural populations (Pujol, 1999; Benedetti, 2015). Inside tango culture, new musical forms questioned the traditional canons of the Golden Age of tango, through artists such as Astor Piazzolla or Eduardo Rovira.

The return to democracy in 1983 led to a reappropriation of the genre by a new generation of musicians. This musical revival involved experimentation, the incorporation of other music genres (such as jazz and rock), and included a search for cultural revivalism. As the Argentinian crisis of 2001 was germinating, tango became an identity haven for some musicians and dancers (Luker, 2007), while the milongas became places of resistance against the deterioration of social ties caused by the expansion of neoliberalism (Liska, 2017). Young artists and practitioners called for the re actualisation of the *tanguero* legacy as an alternative and committed cultural practice, against the hegemonic tendencies of the globalised music industry. As evidenced by the conversion of many rock and roll artists to tango (Daniel Melingo, Limón García, Omar Mollo) (Anad, 2008), this genre became a venue for social protest (Cecconi, 2017). Other actors saw it from a purely artistic point of view or as a professional opportunity, following the development of a tango "for export" within the "tango economic complex" (Kanai, 2014). Interest in tango abroad was reactivated by the presentation of the Tango Argentino show at the Théâtre du

---

[1] Authors' translation: "Distant Buenos Aires, how beautiful you must be! / It's been ten years now since you saw me set sail... / Here, in this Montmartre, a sentimental suburb, / I feel the memory pierce me with its dagger".

Châtelet in Paris in 1983, followed by an international tour that lasted several years. From this standpoint, tango appeared either as a specialised practice or as a touristic show and product, where the music held a very variable place.

2.2 Tango Musicians and DJs

The experience of tango and the importance attributed to the music differ according to the practitioners (dancers, musicians, *tangueros*[2]): music is used as a support for the practice danced in milongas, contributes to the tango shows and tango concerts are organised in the city. The place of the musicians within tango thus appears contrasted, more or less visible depending on the different tango scenes.

In the past, music in milonga venues was mainly played by tango groups or orchestras. The golden years of tango resulted in a concomitant development of orchestras and balls. The tango orchestra was created in 1911. It first took the form of the *sexteto típico*, consisting of two bandoneons, two violins, a piano and a double bass, and later evolved into the *orquesta típica*, with more musicians for bandoneon and violin lines (Plisson, 2004). However, the decrease in attendance at milongas and the diminution of the importance of tango in Argentina from the 1960s onwards led to a considerable reduction in the number of orchestras and their gradual replacement by recorded music (from vinyl records to CDs and next mp3s), for economic reasons (difficulties in remunerating musicians) but also because of a focus on a musical form inherited from the past. Nowadays, in milonga venues, the music is mainly played electronically (primarily mp3s) or, occasionally, using vinyl records. The figure of the DJ then emerged, replacing the milonga organiser who had previously overseen the music selection. DJs are recognised for their skills in ensuring the "musicalisation" of the milonga. They can be house DJs at the same venue, or guest DJs. They are evaluated in relation to their fame within the world of tango, and move around depending on the festivals and their own life paths.

Musicians have not entirely disappeared, however, from the milongas, even though they are no longer a mandatory presence. Groups may perform during a milonga, with the constraint of having to adapt their music

---

[2] Tangueros are passionate about tango, to the point that it permeates their relationship to the world.

to the practice of the dance, before giving way to the DJ for the rest of the ball. Rare milongas operate with a group in residence, such as the orchestra El Afronte in the historic San Telmo district of Buenos Aires, a favourite destination for tourists who are new to tango (the live performance being preceded by tango classes in English and Spanish).

Initiated with Astor Piazzolla in the mid-1950s, the dissociation between tango as a ball and as a musical performance in specialised venues (concert halls) has become more pronounced over the years. Musicians and orchestras perform in concerts or on tour at the various tango festivals in Argentina or elsewhere in the world.

In Buenos Aires, tango musicians also play in another type of venue specific to tourists, namely the *casas del tango*, which offer shows with a troupe of dancers, but also an orchestra,[3] sometimes taking up the structure of the orchestra in residence, and often featuring songs by a male and female duo. The repertoire is standardised, ranging from the early tangos (including *La Cumparsita*) and Gardel's tangos, to more recent compositions by Piazzolla, and even electronic tango. Tango shows are often decried by practitioners as "for export", a fixed form that reproduces a stereotypical and exoticised imaginary of the practice, which produces also in return a specific and stereotypical imaginary of Buenos Aires, as revealed by the analysis of the iconography of tango and of Buenos Aires in tourist guides (Cominelli et al., 2020). Nevertheless, the musicians who perform there are often professionals recognised by their peers, and at the same time develop personal musical projects that they perform in other places (bars, concert halls), sometimes just after having performed in costume for tourists.

This multiplicity of tango music venues goes hand in hand with a specialisation of musical repertoires, with the dominant forms of tango emphasising compositions and arrangements from the past.

2.3 A Repertoire Reminiscent of a Golden Age?

In the traditional milongas, the musical repertoire focuses on around a hundred tangos composed or recorded during the Golden Age of tango, performed by around fifteen renowned orchestras. According to a 2015

---

[3] Casa de tango performances with live music are presented by tourism agencies as being of higher quality than those with recorded music.

4 TANGO MUSIC: BETWEEN HERITAGE AND TRANSNATIONAL RESOURCES... 81

survey on the Facebook page TangoTecnia[4] based on an international panel of 2229 responses, the orchestras most appreciated by the dancers were those of D'Arienzo, Di Sarli, Pugliese, Canaro, Troilo and Caló, all belonging to this Golden Age. The "living" orchestras that topped the rankings were those that replicate the style of a large orchestra, such as the Orquesta Típica la Juan d'Arienzo (12th position) or the orchestra Color Tango, which reproduces the style of Osvaldo Pugliese (19th position). This tendency to reproduce old tangos in milongas poses a problem for musicians who propose contemporary (non-danceable) compositions and who are thus forced to find or invent other performance venues.

To overcome this difficulty, the multiple musical groups that have emerged in Buenos Aires over the last thirty years have reconfigured a local tango scene, structured around a circuit of places located in the city and its surrounding suburbs. Most of the venues for the performance and transmission of the practice are developed outside of the institutional framework, in unconventional places (basements, houses, reclaimed factories), in neighbourhood cultural centres, in bars and sometimes in the street. This alternative circuit maintains a bohemian or industrial aesthetic, like the Club Atlético Fernandez Fierro, the first self-managed tango venue created in 2004 in a warehouse by the Orquesta Típica Fernandez Fierro.

Self-designating their form of tango as "new", "young", "*de ruptura*" ("tango of rupture", representing a complete break with traditional tango music), or contemporary, the musical formations that make up the "new guard" encompass a wide range of aesthetic proposals and vary in terms of instruments and number of musicians.[5] From the second half of the 1980s onwards, the younger generation of groups started out as a duo (often guitar and voice), trio, quartet and quintet, making extensive use of instruments associated with the "old guard" of tango (guitar, flute), whose repertoire was revisited, or in a post-Piazzolla style, with a harmonic research close to jazz or European art music (Polti, 2016). The end of the 1990s saw the development of a movement which aimed to recreate the *orquestas típicas*, and it was led by the orchestras El Arranque (1996) and Fernandez Branca (1999, which later became the Fernandez Fierro orchestra). These

---

[4] Which no longer exists on Facebook. We conducted an interview with the organizer of this survey who lived in Buenos Aires in 2017.

[5] From the figure of the cantautor (a singer, composer, often guitarist) alone on stage, to orchestras of around twenty musicians.

groups engaged in different dialogues with tradition, according to three types (Cecconi, 2017): successors, reformists and those who worked through hybridisation or fusion with other music genres (rock, jazz, Latin American or art music).[6]

This relative dissociation within the practice of tango between places dedicated to dance (the milongas) based on old recordings and places of live musical practice is reflected in the public policies of the development and recognition of tango music, both in Buenos Aires and in Montevideo.

3 Music in Public Policies in Buenos Aires and Montevideo

Inscribed in 2009 on UNESCO's Representative List of the Intangible Cultural Heritage of Humanity, tango is defined as "a genre that originally involved dance, music, poetry and singing. Tango expresses a way of conceiving the world and life and it nourishes the cultural imagery of the inhabitants of the capital cities of the Río de la Plata" (UNESCO, 2009). This inscription represents the culmination of a joint effort by Uruguay and Argentina and gives this practice international visibility. The public policies implemented in both cities struggled to grasp the transversality and porosity of the artistic genres associated with tango and the significance—not only on an economic, but also on a cultural and social level—of this element of Intangible Cultural Heritage. The comparison between Buenos Aires and Montevideo also reveals two strategies undertaken to preserve and promote tango through the importance given to tango music.

3.1 Buenos Aires: Policies for Preserving and Promoting Tango Music

National cultural policies in Argentina in favour of tango date back to the 1970s. In 1977, based on Ben Molar's proposal from 1965, the date of 11th December became National Tango Day, commemorating the birthdays of two emblematic figures of tango music: singer and actor Carlos Gardel (1890) and musician, composer and orchestra conductor Julio de Caro (1899). The Academia Nacional del Tango de la República Argentina (National Tango Academy) was founded on 28th June 1990 upon the

---

[6] Transformations in the music led to discussions on the scope of the genre, particularly with the arrival of electronic tango; see Buch (2014).

initiative of poet and tango historian Horacio Ferrer. The decree creating the Academy highlights the history of tango and its role as an "authentic artistic expression", marking the identity of the Argentinian people and boasting an international reputation. In 2000, the Academy opened a museum dedicated to tango and its history, with a strong emphasis on music. Following the decree of 1990, tango was recognised as national heritage in 1996. The law of 11th December 2014 established a "promotion scheme for notable cafés, bars, billiard halls and tearooms", under the leadership of the Ministry of Culture, to identify and promote notable bars. In some cases, these were places with a long history related to tango and famous tango composers: Homero Manzi, for example, composed the lyrics of several tangos in El Buzón, today a notable bar. In addition to this, the 2009 regulations on the export of bandoneons aim to keep these old, traditional instruments, made more than forty years ago, in the country.

In Buenos Aires, tango was declared as part of the city's heritage in 1998 by municipal law and a tango festival was created that same year. The Carlos Gardel Museum was inaugurated in Buenos Aires in 2003 in the house where the singer had lived with his mother. This house-museum presented the spaces and objects of the musician's daily life. It was reconfigured from 2016 onwards by the Dirección General de Museos de la Ciudad de Buenos Aires, with a museographic project that profoundly reconfigured the space, making greater use of digital resources.

A crucial role is also played by both tourism policies and public and private actions aimed at anchoring tango in its territories of origin and making it a catalyst for tourism. In Argentina, this will has taken the form of territorial marketing policies (Broclain, 2012). With this in mind, the government of the city of Buenos Aires merged the tango festival and the World Tango Championship in 2009 to create TangoBA, a major event of international renown, attracting practitioners and audiences from all over the world, and emphasising the practice of dance more than the music. A tango tourism offer was also developed by private entrepreneurs, with the creation of tango shows in the *Casas de tango* (Madero Tango, Esquina Carlos Gardel, etc.). This tourism offer turns tango into a show where dancers and musicians are hired by an entrepreneur to perform a stereotypical history of tango, from its origins in the seediest parts of Río de la Plata cities to the most famous tangos from all over the world.

The role of tango is also central in urban developments, led by private initiatives and/or public interventions, of emblematic neighbourhoods such as Abasto and La Boca. Here, urban markers (murals, façades, statues) turned these places into open-air galleries (Cominelli et al., 2020). In La Boca, the music played through loudspeakers accompanies the couples dancing in the street, nurturing informal activities around tango tourism, but this atmosphere is also conveyed by the statues, e.g. of bandoneon musicians, reproduced on windows, on balconies and in the streets. A similar, more recent approach can be found in the Abasto district, nearby the site of the Carlos Gardel Museum, where frescoes evoke tango, the singer and the lyrics of his songs.

3.2   Montevideo: Music as a Difference

In Uruguay, cultural policies in favour of the heritage creation of tango are more recent and more importantly subsequent to its inscription on the Representative List of the Intangible Cultural Heritage of Humanity. Unlike in Buenos Aires, tango is not a central theme in the tourism imagination of Montevideo or in the city's tourism policies. Indeed, the *candombe* (also inscribed on the ICH list in 2009) or the carnival (to which a municipal museum is dedicated) are more associated with the city.

The Uruguayan approach positions tango music centrally, both in terms of heritage and promotion, in three ways: highlighting the Uruguayan origins of Carlos Gardel, promoting *La Cumparsita* (the most famous tango in the world), and enhancing the specificity of Uruguayan tango music. Dance is thus less important here than in Buenos Aires, even though tango cabarets and dance shows are organised for cruise tourists with a stopover in Montevideo.

In 2006, the date of 8th October was chosen as National Tango Day, commemorating the date on which Carlos Gardel, a resident of Buenos Aires, took steps to be recognised as a Uruguayan national, declaring Tacuarembó, a city in the north of the country, as his birthplace. A statue in front of the Facal bar, on the main avenue of the city of Montevideo, depicting Gardel seated at a table on the café terrace, was inaugurated in 2015 by the public authorities. The owner of the bar regularly organises tango demonstrations there.

In addition, one of the most famous tangos in the world, *La Cumparsita*, was composed in Montevideo in 1917 by Gerardo Matos Rodríguez. *La Cumparsita* has become the national anthem of tango. It had already been heralded as the "cultural and popular anthem of the Republic of Uruguay" in 1998. In 2017, to mark the centenary of its composition, La Cumparsita

Museum was founded in the Salvo Palace, which had been inaugurated in 1928 on the site of the former *confitería* (tearoom) La Giralda where this tango was first performed. This museum, created by a private individual, brings together a collection of objects that belonged to the composer. Such showcasing of G. Matos Rodríguez and his work can also be seen in the AGADU official archive museum (institution managing author copyright) inaugurated in 1964, with a Matos Rodrídguez collection comprising scores, press articles, his piano and his harmonium occupying half of the museum space. Numerous events paying tribute to *La Cumparsita* have been organised in recent years for international promotion purposes. The National Heritage Day in 2017, for example, was organised around the theme of this tango with numerous activities, concerts and a photo exhibition. The promotional leaflets on tango produced by the Ministry of Tourism also highlight *La Cumparsita* and Gardel, two world-famous tango icons.

Finally, a discourse on the specificity and difference of the Uruguayan form of tango has been developed. The name of the tango school supported by various public institutions, Destaoriya, means "this side of the shore" (of the Río de la Plata), a way of defining itself in relation to Argentina. The school promotes the use of the bandoneon but also the guitar, which is a way of recalling the ancestral nature of Uruguayan tango. Indeed, the *payadores*, musicians from rural areas improvising songs on the guitar, are often considered to be the precursors of tango. The contemporary use of guitars in tango groups is then interpreted as a return to the origins of the practice. José Planchon, Uruguayan guitarist from the group Estilo Re Fa Si, talked in an interview (2019) about the need to defend guitar tango, recalling that before the invention of the great orchestras, the guitar was the dominant instrument used, especially with José María Aguilar. Carlos Gardel himself recorded most of his tangos with guitarists. The promotion of a Uruguayan difference in tango then claims a connection to a form of ancestral customs, which can also be found in Uruguayan dance (Werosch & Veneziani, 2018).

These cultural policies in Buenos Aires and Montevideo demonstrate a particular attention to the music and history of tango, its musical instruments and the places where it is practised, for identity and preservation purposes, but also, increasingly, for the development of tourism. However, their meanings vary between the two cities. In Buenos Aires, these music policies remain dissociated from the dominant tourist promotion centred mainly on dance. For Montevideo, the valorisation of tango music also

86   E. BROCLAIN ET AL.

shows the will to build a differentiated tango identity, less centred on dance, compared to Buenos Aires. Artists and musicians are involved in other preservation actions that are more in line with the register of transmission, the relevant actions are being taken in a balance between reproducing the traditional ways of playing and promoting tango as an art in the making.

3.3   Transmitting Tango Through Practice and Training

Intangible heritage requires actions of transmission for the preservation of a musical heritage composed of scores and a repertoire of ways of playing. This means a variety of intergenerational approaches, for the training of musicians.

In Buenos Aires, one of the driving forces behind the revival of tango music comes from institutions, with the creation of the School of Popular Music of Avellaneda (EMPA) in 1986. Previously, musicians learned tango with other more experienced players by integrating *orquestas típicas*, but this process was interrupted. By calling on leading musicians such as Horacio Salgan (composer and pianist, 1916–2016) or Rodolfo Mederos (bandoneonist, born in 1940), the school participated in the transmission of the gestures of the musical practice, particularly specific instrumental techniques called "*yeites*". Numerous figures of today's tango were trained there and then became teachers, such as the pianist and composer Julian Peralta. This institutionalisation of the teaching of tango music continued in the following years with the opening of a tango section at the Conservatorio Municipal de Música "Manuel de Falla" in 2003 and then at the Conservatorio Superior de Música, renamed "Astor Piazzolla" by decree in 2007. Another issue concerns the preservation of scores, difficult for young musicians to access, and their use for transmission purposes through their collection, digitisation, reproduction and dissemination.

Other initiatives testify to the difficulty of obtaining long-term public commitment. "The flaws in the system" allowed the creation of the Tango Orchestra School by Ignacio Varchausky (interview, 2015). This project arose in 1996 from Varchausky's research as a musician, eager to learn a language with scattered codes. A few surviving musicians from the Golden Age were still performing in local halls or bars,[7] but there was an urgency

---

[7] On the importance of neighbourhood bars as places of mysticism and transmission, see Gubner (2018).

4 TANGO MUSIC: BETWEEN HERITAGE AND TRANSNATIONAL RESOURCES... 87

because the holders of this knowledge were gradually dying out. With the Tango Orchestra School, Varchausky wanted to establish a structure where everyone could learn tango from seven styles (D'Arienzo, De Sarli, Gobbi, Piazzola, Pugliese, Salgan and Troilo), under the supervision of the musicians who had participated in their elaboration. Sponsored by composer and musician Emilio Balcarce (1918–2011), the project was validated in 2000 by Carlos Villalba, director of Buenos Aires Música (the city's cultural secretariat), on the initiative of the first tango festival. The programme still exists today and has trained more than 400 musicians, but at the cost of a constant struggle to keep the orchestra within the local government budget.

This orchestra is just one milestone in the work to preserve tango music in a more advanced way. In 2002, with the help of American jazz trumpeter Wynton Marsallis, Varchausky founded TangoVia Buenos Aires, a non-profit organisation dedicated to the preservation and promotion of tango. In 2009, he presented the Digital Tango Archive, designed to recover lost materials relating to the history of tango recordings. Their work is financed mainly by private donations and a few grants, but as yet no institution has taken over the initiative.

Other musicians have set up self-managed self-training projects. The Maquina Tanguera (1999) was established as a union of *orquestas típicas*, in which musicians trained at EMPA share their knowledge and scores with younger people and stimulate group dynamics by organising concerts and parties, the "*orquestazos*". In 2006, pianist Julian Peralta founded his own school, the Escuela Orlando Goñi, that promotes "*tango de ruptura*". This cooperative is designed to function "as a factory that helps generate and support new *tanguero* musical projects", emphasising innovation and inviting students to create their own compositions and arrangements. The Tango Orchestra School and the Escuela Orlando Goñi are united in their desire to train future musicians, but they advocate two different relationships to tradition.

In Montevideo, the challenge of transmission concerns a smaller number of initiatives and institutions. At the institutional level, dance is the main object of training policies: a tango section has recently been opened within the National School of Dance, justified by the inclusion of tango on the list of Intangible Cultural Heritage. Musical training takes place within the Cienarte Foundation created by Raúl Jaurena, a Uruguayan bandoneonist, with the opening of a tango section in 2007. Operating with limited means, this school was for a long time the only tango training school, with the challenge of going beyond a nostalgic approach to the practice for an "open tango". All instruments are taught, including singing and guitar, presented as emblematic elements of Uruguayan tango. A project co-managed by CIAT and Cienarte, funded by UNESCO in 2020, aims to disseminate bandoneon teaching to young people via free classes and to promote instrument making, in order to ensure the transmission of know-how that will enable these musical instruments to be preserved.

As we will explore it in the last section, it is within this framework, defined by heritage, tourism and tango transmission policies and actions, that the trajectories of practitioners—particularly musicians—have been defined, not only at the level of the cities of the Río de la Plata, but also internationally.

4 Strategies and Movements of Musicians

Musicians implement diverse strategies to bring their music to life and make a living from it. They adapt to different contexts, diversify the places where they perform, acquire new skills and develop various economic strategies. These strategies also involve mobility on various scales, which we will explore through the trajectories of certain tango musicians and actors in Buenos Aires, Montevideo and Paris.

4.1 From the Río de la Plata…

At the local level, tango exists in multiple ways, both in Buenos Aires and Montevideo. Argentinian and Uruguayan musicians often encounter it through family ties, in the vinyl records belonging to their parents or grandparents: "*I have been playing the guitar since I was 13 years old. My grandmother liked tango, and in my family's neighbourhood, my guitar teacher taught me some tangos*" (Augustin, Buenos Aires 2018). Tango can also be learned through public or private institutions: "*My dad thought I had to play the violin, so I started to play at eight. I began at the Conservatory, first national then municipal […] but I didn't feel comfortable with the formal study so I quit when I was about 14 years old, and continued playing with youth orchestras*" (Lucas, Buenos Aires 2017).

The musicians stress the need to bring to life a music rooted in the culture of the Río de la Plata. This does not only mean learning and reproducing tango music, but also renewing and innovating it. The places where musicians perform are multiple and require a permanent adaptation of repertoires, styles and training. To ensure a regular stage and to conquer a public of dancers, some musicians organise their own milongas, such as the Sexteto Fantasma in the milonga Ventanita de Arrabal, or the orchestra El Afronte, which has been managing the Maldita milonga for more than ten years: "*we needed a space to play, not only to attract dancers, because they can also go to milongas where they play old music, but precisely to understand the importance of live music, to sustain a genre, the important thing being that the dancers listen and dance to new music*" (Lucas, El Afronte, Buenos Aires 2017). The milonga is thus experienced as a place where tango music is played, evolves and expresses itself in connection with the ball and the dancers: "*I like it a bit more when it's a concert, but also, on the other hand, I like to play in some milongas because it generates something nice, in terms of communication with the people who dance*" (Augustin Luna, Buenos Aires 2018). Some musicians declare the importance of learning to dance in order to better understand the music and the needs of the dancers, in a world of milongas marked by the domination of recorded music: "*dancing generates a different relationship to the music, both in the way it is played and in the structure. For example, the question of, when you're at a ball, the order in which you play the tangos is quite an important factor*" (Romain De Mesmay, Orquesta Silbando, Paris 2016).

The *Casas de tango*, other emblematic places for the activity of musicians, are part of an economic strategy and not an artistic research, as it has happened in other music tourist destinations such as in New Orleans (Atkinson, 1997). With the exception of certain shows, working conditions are often precarious and salaries unattractive, but the *Casas* do offer regular income for a relatively low number of hours (14 to 21 hours per week), allowing the musicians to devote themselves to other projects. In addition, they enrol the musicians in a professional network that gives them access to other resources (international tours with shows for export, private concerts in embassies, in the homes of wealthy individuals or for companies, etc.): "*We had our presence in Japan. Together with maestro Lazzari, a producer came from Japan to our Casa and took him to Japan. […] We have sold our shows in so many places*" (*Casa de tango* La Ventana, Buenos Aires 2018).

This link between local practice and international mobilities is also asserted within festivals, in particular the Buenos Aires international festival, which target mostly tourists. Some musicians point out that this is the only event where the city directly allocates significant resources to the promotion of tango. However, according to some of them, the orchestras showcased are often similar, although the organisers have started to program new musicians with different practices. *"Very recently, the festival programmers started to look for new musicians coming from our environment. This helped several of us to participate in the festival. (...)"* (Lucas, Buenos Aires 2017). Musicians' strategies thus follow artistic, economic, but also political logics, which can be expressed through their refusal to take part in a world-famous public event as a sign of protest against a government that, they consider, does not support them as artists.

Other festivals are organised by tango activists who aspire instead to highlight the social role of the practice. For instance, the Festival de Tango Independiente was initiated in 2010 to protest against the commodification of the official festival and to showcase the current and underground scene, first in Buenos Aires, then in other Argentinian cities and in Montevideo. This experience led to the organisation of numerous neighbourhood festivals (in La Boca, Almagro, Boedo, etc.) organised by local actors, whose aim was to show the tango in its diversity to a wider public and to bring it to places the official festival wasn't reaching: *"street concerts, more concerts in schools, more concerts in places, as we say, in situations of social emergency"* (Ildefonso Pereyra, Buenos Aires 2018).

Tango musicians thus cross the family world, the world of formal and informal education, the world of milongas, *Casas de tango* and concert venues. In these worlds, with porous borders, musical practice is transmitted and evolves, without being fixed. These local mobilities also demonstrate the complexity of the geographies of tango in cities, and the strategies implemented by musicians who perform in extremely different and sometimes conflicting places, adapting their practice according to these places and their audiences. It is the richness of these experiences in places emblematic of tango that seems to contribute to strengthening the "capital of autochthony" (Retière, 2003) of musicians. This Bourdieusian-inspired notion was originally designed to stress the importance of the resources linked to local roots and sociabilities and helps to understand how the origins along the Río de la Plata confer to musicians an added value that enables them to go from local to international mobilities. We can thus speak of a process of legitimation (Boltanski & Esquerre, 2017) which, thanks to the reputation acquired, helps musicians to become part of the "elites" who circulate internationally.

Is this legitimisation through autochthony a claim to musical authenticity? In addition to being defined in relation to a "here", authenticity and legitimacy are also constructed in relation to an "elsewhere" (Guillard &

Sonnette, 2020). This legitimisation through autochthony, including in a situation of mobility, also comes up against the globalisation of tango music, resulting in different dynamics of authentication that can compete with each other: local and translocal authentication (Elafros, 2013), as shown by the global trajectories of musicians from the Rio de la Plata, but also by tango musical creation in other places, notably in France. Although circulating musicians claim a filiation with Buenos Aires and the Río de la Plata, they also inscribe themselves in geographical universes of reference that represent local regimes of authenticity (Guillard & Sonnette, 2020). The relationship to the original home of tango then appears more ambiguous, between imitation and differentiation.

4.2 ...to the Worlds of Tango

The movement of tango musicians is not a recent phenomenon. The transnational dimension of tango has been present since its origins, as evidenced by the round trips between Paris and Buenos Aires since the beginning of the twentieth century (Zalko, 2004). Whether to Madrid or to Paris, on board transatlantic liners, musicians moved around, as did tango scores. Some musicians, who settled in Paris as early as 1907, opened publishing houses and recorded several tango records there. The titles circulated towards Buenos Aires with an aura of added legitimacy after a passage through the European music halls. According to Nardo Zalko, tango has always been part of the Parisian soundscape: "It has been here for a century and has never left" (Zalko, 2004, p. 275).

The revival of tango in the 1980s was linked to world tours of tango shows (notably Tango Argentino), and brought about a new globalisation of the practice. Subsequent movements to Buenos Aires took place according to tourist logics (to discover the original spaces of tango) or training logics (to take classes or workshops). From Buenos Aires (and to a lesser extent Montevideo), centrifugal logics also served to export tango abroad, with historical anchor points (Paris, Berlin, Istanbul or New York) or other more recent ones, diversifying their destinations. In return, tango experiences from all over the world now enrich the music and practice of tango in the Río de la Plata.

The interviews conducted allow us to identify these movements and how they affect the music and practice of tango. Whether they are seasonally mobile or permanently settled, Argentinian expatriates vary their activities, especially in terms of dance. Generally, tango teachers also organise milongas, workshops, festivals and set up troupes, companies and shows. They act as an invitation relay for other maestros who tour the milongas in Europe or North America, where during the summer months they move from one festival to another.

These movements also involve musicians, who perform during tours or at festivals, as shown by the example of tango festivals in France. Some French festivals (Tangopostale in Toulouse, Paris Banlieues Tango, etc.) sometimes program a concert every evening (the Tarbes en Tango festival in the south-west of France) with groups and musicians from Argentina, but also from France or other countries (interviews conducted in 2020, ICH sheet). Some "fashionable" tango orchestras (such as the Sexteto Milonguero, La Juan D'Arienzo or Romantica Milonguera) are often invited to several festivals in France and throughout Europe. The size of the invited orchestras nevertheless incurs a significant financial cost for festival organisers, who seek to pool their attendance with other venues, or suggest that the musicians attend in a reduced formation (quintet or quartet). These festivals are also places for training and transmission, particularly in Tarbes, thanks to master classes dedicated to instruments of the *orquesta típica*, to guitar or singing, but also to improvisation (*a la parilla*) (interview with Chloé Pfeiffer, Paris 2018). In addition to the Conservatoire de Gennevilliers in the Parisian suburbs (the only one with a tango department), the training of French tango musicians seems to involve encounters with Argentinian musicians passing through France, as Romain, who has followed several courses and workshops with Fernando Maguna's Orquesta Típica de Marseille, explained to us. These festivals then encourage the development of a French tango music scene, partly professionalised (some French tango musicians have the status of entertainment workers, and others among those interviewed have another job at the same time). The festivals become "a real hub" for musicians who create a network, and in turn invest in transmission. Chloé, a professional musician, organises workshops in Tarbes and has created La Típica Paris with Roger Helou, an orchestra offering workshops for more experienced musicians (interview with Chloé Pfeiffer).

These international movements of musicians and the encounters and networks formed have an influence on tango music and its variations. The French musicians interviewed mention a hybridisation of musical styles, through a reinterpretation of the classic tango repertoires in the light of very different styles such as those of French *chanson* or film music, as shown by the Armenonville project, which defines itself as "a tango music group always on the move". According to one of the musicians, R. de Mesmay, "*At Armenonville, the idea is to mix Argentinian tangos and tangos from French chanson. We create a repertoire, integrating a Russian tango or tangos from film music*" (interview 2017). These gatherings and hybridisations, accentuated by the encounters between musicians from different geographical horizons, in Buenos Aires (through the mobility of musicians from all over the world who attend classes or orchestra school sessions there) or elsewhere, lead to the creation and reinterpretation of tango music.

5   CONCLUSION

Tango music, perceived as a nostalgic territorialised experience and as a poetic and musical heritage, is today confronted with contrasting evolutions on several different scales.

Tango as music is a heritage component in its own right, the object of a safeguarding policy based on commemorative laws, inventories allowing its preservation and the creation of museums. Texts, lyrics, melodies, scores and instruments are major elements of the tango museums of Buenos Aires and Montevideo. However, these policies are disconnected from the tourism development encouraged by public policies that participate in the highlighting of tango shows and encourage dance and tango for export. The other component of heritage preservation, the transmission of music, is ensured only by orchestra schools and private initiatives. Nevertheless, the porosity is great, and the movements of musicians are numerous between the official fields of promotion and development of tango and the more popular and social manifestations of this art.

A gap exists between the attachment to the standards of the Golden Age of tango, particularly by the milonga dancers, and a renewal of tango linked to issues of contemporary musical creation, driven by external influences and new musical forms, often mixed. Tango orchestras and groups, increasingly numerous, seek to meet the dual challenge of innovating while giving satisfaction to the milonga dancers, multiply the places of their practice, renewing with the milongas and are present in festivals all over the world. The circulation of the music, which has accompanied round trips between Buenos Aires and Paris since the beginning of the twentieth century, now extends throughout the world, carried by a

94 E. BROCLAIN ET AL.

community of musicians with a high level of mobility, broadening the geographical horizons of the transmission and creation of tango music, but also its preservation.

REFERENCES

Anad, G. (2008). La Nueva Guarida del Tango. *Portal: Journal of Multidisciplinary and International Studies, 5*(1). https://doi.org/10.5130/portal.v5i1.482

Apprill, C. (2016). Patrimonialisation de la danse tango: une « tradition » au prisme de sa déterritorialisation. *Autrepart, 78–79*(2–3), 145–162.

Atkinson, C. Z. (1997). Whose New Orleans? Music's place in the packaging of New Orleans for tourism. In S. Abram, D. MacLeod, & J. Waldren (Eds.), *Tourists and tourism: Identifying with people and places* (pp. 91–106). Routledge.

Benedetti, H. (2015). *Nueva historia del tango: De los orígenes al siglo XXI*. Siglo Veintiuno Editores.

Boltanski, L., & Esquerre, A. (2017). *Enrichissement: une critique de la marchandise*. Gallimard.

Broclain, E. (2012). Tango®. Enjeux d'une stratégie de promotion territoriale fondée sur la réappropriation d'un patrimoine musical. *Questions de communication, 22*, 123–140.

Buch, E. (2014). Gotan Project's Tango Project. In M. Miller (Ed.), *Tango lessons: Movement, sound, image, and text in contemporary practice* (pp. 220–242). Duke University Press.

Canova, N. (2013). Music in French geography as space marker and place maker. *Social & Cultural Geography, 14*(8), 861–867.

Cecconi, S. (2017). La crisis de 2001 y el tango juvenil: de la protesta política y social a las formas alternativas de organización y expresión. *Estudios sociológicos, 35*, 103.

Cohen, S., Roberts, L., Knifton, R., & Leonard, M. (2015). Introduction: Locating popular music heritage. In R. Cohen & L. Knifton (Eds.), *Sites of popular music heritage, memories, histories, places* (pp. 1–11). Routledge.

Cominelli, F., Jacquot, S., & Salin, E. (2020). Iconographies et imaginaires du tango, entre circulations et hybridations. In M. Gravari-Barbas (Ed.), *Le patrimoine mondial, mise en tourisme, mise en images* (pp. 173–194). L'Harmattan.

Connell, J., & Gibson, C. (2002). *Sound tracks, popular music, identity and place*. Routledge.

Elafros, A. (2013). Greek hip hop: Local and translocal authentication in the restricted field of production. *Poetics, 41*(1), 75–95.

Gervais-Lambony, P. (2012). Nostalgies citadines en Afrique Sud. EspacesTemps. net. https://www.espacestemps.net/articles/nostalgies-citadines-en-afrique-sud/.

Gibson, C., & Connell, J. (2005). *Music and tourism, On the road again*. Channel View Publications.

Gubner, J. (2018). More than Fishnets & Fedoras: Filming social aesthetics in the neighborhood Tango scenes of Buenos Aires & The Making of A Common Place (2010). *Sound Ethnographies, 1*(1), 171–186.

Guillard, S., & Sonnette, M. (2020). Légitimité et authenticité du hip-hop: rapports sociaux, espaces et temporalités de musiques en recomposition. *Volume !, 17*(2). https://doi.org/10.4000/volume.8482

Kanai, M. (2014). Buenos Aires, capital of Tango: tourism, redevelopment and the cultural politics of neoliberal urbanism. *Urban Geography, 35*(8), 1111–1117.

Lashua, B., Spracklen, K., & Long, P. (2014). Introduction to the special issue: Music and tourism. *Tourist Studies, 14*(1), 3–9.

Liska, M. (2017). *Argentine queer Tango: Dance and sexuality politics in Buenos Aires*. Lexington Books.

Luker, M. J. (2007). Tango renovación: On the uses of music history in post-crisis Argentina. *Latin American Music Review / Revista de Música Latinoamericana, 28*(1), 68–93.

Machin-Autenrieth, M. (2015). Flamenco ¿AlgoNuestro? (Something of ours?): Music, regionalism and political geography in Andalusia, Spain. *Ethnomusicology Forum, 24*(1), 4–27.

Peterson, R., & Bennett, A. (2004). Introducing music scenes. In A. Bennett & R. Peterson (Eds.), *Music scenes: Local, translocal and virtual*. Vanderbilt University Press.

Plisson, M. (2004). *Tango, du noir au blanc*. Cité de la Musique / Arles: Actes Sud.

Polti, V. (2016). Nuevos Tangos en Buenos Aires. Diálogos intergenéricos, porosidad e identidades compartidas. In M. Liska & S. Venegas (Eds.), *Tango Ventanas del Presente II: De la gesta a la historia musical reciente*. Desde la Gente, IMFC.

Pujol, S. (1999). *Historia del baile. De la milonga a la disco*. Emecé Editores.

Retière, J.-N. (2003). Autour de l'autochtonie. Réflexions sur la notion de capital social populaire. *Politix, 16*(63), 121–143.

Törnqvist, M. (2013). *Tourism and the globalization of emotions, the intimate economy of Tango*. Routledge.

UNESCO, Candidature pour l'inscription sur la Liste représentative en 2009, référence 00258, Argentine-Uruguay. Le Tango. Présenté à la 4e session à Baou Dhabi. 15 p.

Werosch, S., & Veneziani, W. (2018). *Abran cancha, aca baila un oriental. El Tango de los uruguayos*. Ediciones del Oso.

Zalko, N. (2004). *Paris Buenos Aires, Un siècle de tango*. Editions du Félin.

CHAPTER 5

Taking Music to the (Museum) Masses: Museum Engagement with the Country and Grunge Music Heritages of Nashville and Seattle

Christina Ballico

Abstract In recent decades there has been an increased interest in popular music's role and contribution to heritage, its engagement within museum settings and in turn, its capacity to drive tourism. This chapter examines genre- and place-specific music tourism as it relates to two large-scale cultural institutions—the Country Music Hall of Fame and Museum and the Museum of Popular Culture—in the North American cities of Nashville, Tennessee, and Seattle, Washington, respectively. In doing so, it considers the rich genre-specific popular music heritages of each city—country and grunge—and explores the ways in which this heritage is leveraged within

C. Ballico (✉)
Department of Music, School of Language, Literature, Music and Visual Culture, University of Aberdeen, Aberdeen, UK

Queensland Conservatorium Research Centre, Griffith University, Brisbane, QLD, Australia
e-mail: christina.ballico@abdn.ac.uk

© The Author(s), under exclusive license to Springer Nature   97
Singapore Pte Ltd. 2024
S. Guillard et al. (eds.), *New Geographies of Music 2*, Geographies of Media, https://doi.org/10.1007/978-981-97-2072-9_5

98   C. BALLICO

each institution. In turn, it considers the positioning of music within official tourism campaigns of the city, and through an exploration of their curatorial practices and their positioning with clusters of activity, demonstrates the capacity for each to contribute dynamic music tourism experiences in their respective locales.

Keywords Music history • Music museums • Music tourism • Music heritage

1   INTRODUCTION

In recent decades there has been an increased interest in popular music's role and contribution to heritage, its engagement within museum settings and in turn, its capacity to drive tourism (Baker et al., 2016, 2018; Fairchild, 2017; Gibson & Connell, 2005; Leonard, 2007, 2010; Pirrie Adams, 2015). Considering this, this chapter examines the inclusion of genre- and artist-specific popular music heritages at two North American cultural institutions: The Country Music Hall of Fame and Museum, Nashville, and the Museum of Popular Culture, Seattle. Contextualized within the genre- and place-specific histories of country and grunge in Nashville and Seattle respectively, as well as the prominence of music tourism in these two cities, this chapter examines the Country Music Hall of Fame and Museum and Museum of Popular Music Culture in relation to two factors: (1) their location within downtown clusters of music and/or related cultural institutions and (2) the inclusion and exhibiting of music and associated ephemera in their displays. In doing so, the case for popular music as a cultural good worthy of museum inclusion is furthered, as is the capacity for such inclusion to preserve and perpetuate genre- and place-specific music heritages and associated music tourism activities. This chapter draws on site visits undertaken as part of a cross-US trip in April 2018. In undertaking these site visits the author considered the following: each institution's location within their downtown districts (both broadly and in relation to other arts- and entertainment-engaged institutions); the physical footprint and prominence of the institutions; and the ways in which music was incorporated into their collections, including specifics as to how it was displayed, and artists/genres of note featured. As such, this chapter bridges the gap while also building upon a wealth of research which has examined the curatorial practices and challenges associated engaging popular music in museum settings, and that which has explored the development of downtown entertainment districts which include music museums in their remit (Baker et al., 2016, 2018; Bennett & Rogers, 2016; Fairchild, 2017; Johansson, 2010; Leonard, 2007, 2010; Pirrie Adams, 2015).

An overview of literature examining popular music's engagement in museum spaces is first presented. This includes an exploration of the curatorial decision-making processes, challenges associated with, and critiques of, engaging contemporary music within a museum or similar settings. Considering the high-profile nature of the two institutions examined in this chapter, as well as the vital role of place-based music scenes in shaping the curatorial decisions made within them, attention is then turned to the concepts of music and place and music tourism. A detailed background of the country and grunge music histories in Nashville and Seattle is then presented alongside a consideration of music tourism's role within these cities. A closer exploration of the histories and curatorial practices of Country Music Hall of Fame and Museum and the Museum of Popular Culture is then presented with a particular focus on their capacity to preserve and perpetuate their respective genre and place-specific music scenes and associated music tourism.

2   RESEARCH CONTEXT AND LITERATURE REVIEW

2.1   *Popular Music and the Museum*

Over the last four decades there has been a marked increase in the inclusion of popular (and more broadly contemporary) music within both permanent and temporary exhibits in museums around the world. This has ranged from the establishment of artist-specific museums such as The Beatles Story in Liverpool (in 1990), and the Ramones Museum in Berlin (in 2005), to genre-specific museums such as the New Orleans Jazz Museum in New Orleans (in 1981), the Texas Music Museum in Austin (in 1984), and the Rock n Roll Hall of Fame in Cleveland (in 1995). Artist-specific temporary exhibits have also emerged in more recent decades, such as *David Bowie Is* (which toured globally between 2013 and 2018), and *Exhibitionism: The Rolling Stones* (which toured globally between 2016–2024, being rebranded *The Rolling Stones: Unzipped* in 2021). In other cases—such as the Motown Museum in Detroit—buildings which once housed record label offices and/or recording studios now operate as museums. The capacity for these institutions and exhibits to be established and maintained requires ongoing support from musicians, music fans, city councils, and music organizations. Such support—often focused on financial (pledges, donations, and entrance fees) and material (memorabilia and ephemera) aspects—also influences the scale, scope, and focus of both the collections and associated exhibits as well as the capacity for audience engagement.

The inclusion of popular music in museum and related settings create new ways for music fans to engage with music histories, ephemera, and associated memorabilia which they otherwise would not have had access to while curatorial decisions consider a range of factors relating to taste, popularity, and material accessibility (Leonard, 2007). Significantly, however, engagement with such exhibits relies heavily on the socially constructed nostalgia and remembrance music fans bring to their engagement with such exhibits (Baker et al., 2018; Leonard, 2007, 2018). Arguably, as Pirrie Adams (2015, p. 114) puts forth, engagement with music fans sits at the heart of the music museum and associated exhibits and therefore its,

> audience often comes with a passionate and informed understanding of the subject... the collections of the popular music museum are familiar and frequently solidly and self-evidently connected to interpretive frameworks and social categories.

The opportunity for music fans to engage with music histories in this manner is increasing in importance as historically significant sites of music creation and dissemination continue to be lost through gentrification. In cities such as New York for example, seminal punk music venues such as CBGB and the Fillmore East are now a clothing store and combined bank/apartment complex respectively, while the Hit Factory recording studios is now an upscale apartment complex. That said, while these sites have changed in function, there is a level of memorializing to commemorate their musical heritage. The interior of the John Varvatos clothing store, for example, has maintained much of the character of CBGB, while commemorative photos and plaques are on display in the foyer and on the outside of the building of the now Emigrant Bank, which once housed the Filmore, and the Hit Factory sign remains on prominent display on the outside of the now apartment complex (Atlas Obscura, n.d.). Museum-based music collections and displays are also important in cases of place-based music histories which exist in otherwise suburban locations. Austin, for example, is a city in which much of its contemporary musical history is largely hidden from view, as a result of its continued urbanization. While a range of plaques and statues—commemorating Austin City Limits broadcasts, country musician Willie Nelson and blues guitarist Stevie Ray Vaughn—are scattered in and around the downtown area, much of the music history of the city is not memorialized in a significant manner, nor are many sites of musical significance located in the downtown area. To this end, the community/volunteer run Texas Music Museum provides an opportunity to learn about the music histories of Texas. In other instances, music museums can provide a connection to a localized music history when music tourism is primarily centered on attendance at ephemeral events such as live music performances and festivals. New Orleans, Louisiana, for example, has a rich history associated with jazz music and while the city is home to a range of monuments, statues and public parks commemorating a range of notable jazz musicians, much of the city's music tourism is focused on attendance at ephemeral events such as the New Orleans Jazz and Heritage Festival, Mardi Gras, and the French Quarter Festival. The New Orleans Jazz Museum, however, provides a consistent year-round anchor to the city's rich musical history.

2.2   Challenges and Limitations of Popular Music in the Museum

While music museums make significant contributions to the perpetuating of the musical legacies of the cities in which they operate, it is important to address the challenges and limitations of incorporating music in a museum setting, and broad criticisms levelled against the museum sector. Criticized for their prioritizing of dominant cultural discourses, and in turn in furthering colonialism (Giblin et al., 2019), the sector is currently facing increased pressure to actively decolonize their spaces, reflect a more diverse and inclusive voice and to return artefacts to the cultures and communities from which they were forcibly taken (Farago, 2015; Hunt, 2019; Shoenberger, 2020; Tsjeng, 2020). While music-specific museums have not faced the same level of scrutiny and pressure as the broader museum sector, there have been calls for them to ensure collections are representative of the achievements of women and people of color (Greene, 2021).

102   C. BALLICO

In addition, the inclusion of specific musicians and/or scenes in museum settings has also been criticized by their very members. To mark the 40th anniversary of punk in 2016, for example, the year-long Punk London festival was staged across the city. Both the festival and specific elements within it—such as the British Library's *Punk 1976–78* exhibit—were criticized for being both the antithesis of punk and for the exclusion of women. Joe Corre, son of the Sex Pistols' manager, Malcolm McLaren, responded to the festival by burning punk memorabilia said to be worth GBP5M, proclaiming that "Punk was never, never meant to be nostalgic—and you can't learn how to be one at a Museum of London workshop" (BBC, 2016). Viv Albertine of The Slits defaced *Punk 1976–78* signage replacing the names of all male groups with the names of female-led groups, and signing off with "What about women!!" (Bulut, 2016). In addition, as Leonard (2007, p.147) explains popular music's intersection with museum settings results in,

> debates about historiography, representation, and the ascription of value. Critics have even questioned the appropriateness of placing such music within a museum environment arguing that the tendency of museums to isolate and reify material goes against the dynamic, experiential, transient and often anti-establishment nature of popular music cultures.

Furthermore, access to artefacts and the capacity for specific elements—such as sound and music—to be included in displays further impact the capacity for music histories to be adequately represented in the museum. In addition, music museums expect audiences to be "active, productive and often expert in the knowledge that they bring to such exhibitions" (Leonard, 2010, p. 172). This is not to say that music museums do not engage in educational functions similar to traditional museums (cf Fairchild, 2017), however there is a particularly strong reliance on socially constructed nostalgia in order to have an impact on their audiences. As Pirrie Adams (2015, p. 115) explains, the challenge for popular music museums is not one of *attracting* audiences, but of being able to create an *effective dialogue* with them.

Furthermore, the very nature of the museum exhibit—a curation and reimagination of a performance, event, artist biography, or history through the curation of artefacts (such as stage costumes, awards, handwritten lyrics, and instruments) and media (audio and/or visual recordings of songs)—is by its very nature decontextualizing. As Baker et al. (2016,

p. 71) explain, certain critiques (particularly that of Reynolds, 2011) of the inclusion of music within the museum argue that when,

> ripped from their original context, and transported to the logic of the museum, the inaudible, non-musical artefacts that remain as traces of music's (in)audible past are deficient representations of, or points of access to, that past... [meaning] that all that can be displayed are the extraneous elements of popular music consumption and production; material objects that have lost any use value they had; artefacts that can only hint at the authenticity of experience offered by the sonic encounter.

Furthermore, structuring dimensions such as place can also be problematic as "it risks overstating the significance of place in the cultural biography of an artist or genre" (Baker et al., 2018, p. 8). When considering place as a framing dimension in relation to music museums which capitalize on this in their exhibits however, it is useful to consider the role of music tourism in their functioning.

2.3 Music Tourism

Sitting at the juncture of both heritage and tourism industries, music tourism leverages socially constructed feelings of nostalgia, authenticity, and the mythologizing of place-based music industries and scenes (Fairchild, 2018; Connell & Gibson, 2003; Gibson & Connell, 2005). The association of musicians with specific locations (such as The Beatles with Liverpool) or the notoriety of sites of musical creation and dissemination (such as Abbey Road Studios in London, and Electric Ladyland Studios and CBGB in New York) can act as a driver for music tourism beyond official tourism campaigns (Gibson & Connell, 2005). In some cases, cottage industries of privately run music history tours can also support engagement with place-specific music histories (cf Baker et al., 2016; Friedlander, 2018).

As a result of the emergence of the global Music Cities movement, music tourism is increasingly recognized for its capacity to drive economic development and to support the functioning of broader localized place-based music industries and scenes (Ballico & Watson, 2020; Terrill et al., 2015). Music museums can make significant contributions to the success of this by leveraging their own genre- and place-specific music heritages.

104   C. BALLICO

Doing so can be further bolstered through being located within both entertainment (or similar) districts and mutually beneficial clusters of similar and/or related activities (Cooke & Huggins, 2004; Harper et al., 2015; Johansson, 2010)

3   PLACE-SPECIFIC POPULAR MUSIC HERITAGE AND TOURISM: A NASHVILLE AND SEATTLE COMPARATIVE CASE STUDY

The cities of Nashville and Seattle have played significant roles in the genre-specific music scenes of country and grunge, respectively. Such roles vary in scope and enduring legacy, resulting from differing scales of activity, associated infrastructure, and the timelines of these musical movements. This section unpacks these legacies to demonstrate the varying roles music tourism plays in each of these cities and in turn, the capacity for the Country Music Hall of Fame and Museum and the Museum of Popular Culture to support this. It considers the ways in which country and grunge music legacies exist in both historical and present-day contexts, the status and size of their associated music industrial complexes, the clustering of key sites of activity in and around these institutions, and the role of music tourism in each of the city's official tourism campaigns.

3.1   Nashville, Country Music and Tourism

Nashville's association with country music dates back more than a century, predating even the use of genre label "country" music—and endures to this day as a result of the city's active country music industrial complex. This complex encompasses multitude institutions ranging from those of a creative (recording and song writing studios), cultural (music-engaged museums, live performance venues, and country-music centric television and radio stations), and business (record label offices) nature. Music-related tourism sits at the heart of the city's cultural identity, as evidenced by the prominence of the "Music City" branding and the "Visit Music City" campaign within the city's official tourism campaigns. Commercial tourism operations are also significant in Nashville, with operators such as the Gaylord Entertainment Company (GEC) who own and operate various high-profile live music venues, and resorts in the city such as the Grand Ole Opry, the Ryman Auditorium, and Opryland USA. These tourism campaigns and commercial activities work to leverage a combination of the city's rich country music history and its present-day activities, which for tourists is primarily focused on engaging with live music performances (such as the Grand Ole Opry, the Ryman Auditorium, Bluebird Café, and honky-tonk bars), tours of historical sites (such as Historical RCA Studio B), and attendance at institutions such as the Country Music Hall of Fame and Museum.

Given its rich country music history, Nashville is home to a range of globally recognized live music venues such as the Ryman Auditorium, the Grand Ole Opry, and the Bluebird Café, all of which are highly regarded by musicians and audiences alike as those at which they wish to play and those they seek to attend. Performing at or being invited to be a member of the Grand Ole Opry for example is considered a career milestone (Opry, 2021), while performing at the Bluebird Café is viewed as a rite of passage for Nashville-based musicians and songwriters alike. Indicative of the interplay between sites of activity, not only are there elements of concentrated ownership—as evidenced with GEC—but numerous key sites of activity are also clustered within the city's downtown core, particularly in and around Lower Broadway. As displayed in Fig. 5.1, Lower Broadway is a multiple-block stretch within the Historical Broadway District and is home to numerous honky-tonk bars which play host to a wide array of performances. Other significant country music attractions are also located only a block or two away. The Ryman for example—affectionately known as the "Mother Church" of country music and the original home of the Grand Ole Opry where it operated between 1943 and 1974 before

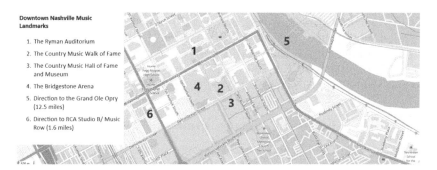

Fig. 5.1 Downtown Nashville Music Landmarks. (Source: Map by the author. Base map: openstreetmap)

relocating approximately 12.5 miles away to the Grand Ole Opry House at Opryland (Ryman Auditorium, 2021)—is located one block away from Broadway, with the Country Music Hall of Fame and Museum and the Country Music Walk of Fame two blocks away. A range of trolley and walking tours operate in and around this district, and through a partnership between the museum and the Mike Curb Family Trust, museum attendees can also participate in guided tours of the Historic RCA Studio B, located in Music Row, approximately 1.6 miles from Lower Broadway. Included in the cost of admission is a bus transfer between the two sites (HRCASB, 2020). The city's tourism office (which has a shop front location inside the Bridgestone Arena) also sells a Music City Total Access Pass—tickets which can be redeemed for access to music-related attractions and tours around the city. Taken collectively, the clustering of sites of activity in the downtown area and the support of the city's tourism office, Nashville's country music history and heritage is highly visible and accessible to tourists.

Owing to its country music heritage, Nashville has also been memorialized by way of the *Nashville* television show. The show, which aired between 2012 and 2018, was filmed at various locations around in Nashville including Grand Ole Opry House (both the main stage and onsite sound stages), and the Ryman Auditorium, while a purpose-built replication of the Bluebird Café was also used. Downtown locations in and around Lower Broadway also featured heavily on the program. *Nashville* had a significant impact on the city's music tourism, with one 2014 study finding that one in five tourists who visited the city were motivated by the television show. In turn, these tourists stayed in the city longer than those who did not visit as a result of the show, and spent 23% more money while visiting (Hodak, 2015; IMDB, n.d.). Each year between 2015 and 2019, the Country Music Hall of Fame and Museum, RCA Studio B, and Hatch Print Show (located within the Museum) collectively welcomed a combined total of upwards of 1,000,000 visitors each year, while in 2015 alone 15 million people visited Nashville (CMHOFM, 2020c; Harper et al., 2015).

3.2   Seattle, Grunge Music, and Tourism

Activities associated with Seattle's grunge music scene are primarily focused on a relatively short period of time—being the late 1980s through the mid-1990s—and on a relatively small number of key artists. Grunge music, while having a significant and enduring impact on global contemporary music popularity trends it is not a genre label applied to present day artists. Instead, it is used to describe music created by a particular group of artists who emerged from a particular urban locale at a particular point in time and who were often signed to a particular record label, being Sub Pop. To this end, the music industrial complex in Seattle is of a much smaller scale than that of Nashville. Certainly, while the city is still home to the Sub Pop offices, and venues notable to the grunge scene such as The Crocodile, The Showbox Market, and the Re-bar are still in operation, grunge was a musical movement which was never supported in the city by prominent large-scale capital infrastructure. This is despite the genre's global impact and memorialization in films such as *Singles* (1992), and the feature length documentary *Hype!* (1996). Its legacy is not promoted as more significant than other tourism categories promoted by the city (such as sightseeing, outdoor activities, events, cultural heritage, and outdoor activities), however the city's official tourism website features details on how to undertake a self-guided grunge history tour of the city (Whiting, 2021). Inclusive of commercial partnerships with several key venues, the instructions for this self-guided tour do not include visiting attractions such as the 1969 Black Sun sculpture in Volunteer Park (the inspiration of the name of Soundgarden's song *Black Hole Sun*), the site of Kurt Cobain's death in the Capitol Hill neighborhood, nor the apartment building featured in the *Singles* film. To this end, while some fan-run driving-based tours are in operation—which allow fans to visit these and other notable sites—engagement with grunge's heritage is heavily reliant on significant prior knowledge of the scene. Considering this, one site which does provide an ease of access to Seattle's music history, and particularly that of grunge, is the Museum of Popular Culture. As illustrated on Fig. 5.2, the museum is located in the Uptown Arts District among a cluster of arts, education, and science focused institutions including the Space Needle, Pacific Science Center, and indie radio station KEXP. The Seattle Arena is also nearby (Seattle Centre, n.d.). Between the years 2016 and 2019, the museum welcomed an average of 734,000 visitors each year (MoPOP, 2017, 2018, 2019, 2020b).

108   C. BALLICO

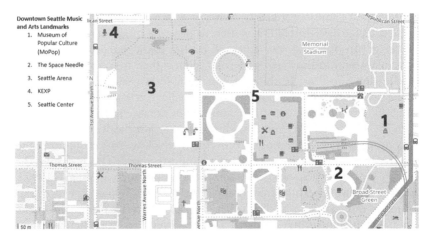

Fig. 5.2 Downtown Seattle Music and Arts Landmarks. (Source: Map by the author. Base map: Openstreetmap)

4   Music Tourism and the Museum: The Country Music Hall of Fame and Museum and The Museum of Popular Culture

Nashville and Seattle not only have rich popular music heritages, but varying scales to which music tourism is officially supported in their cities. It is interesting, therefore, to consider the ways in which large-scale cultural institutions such as the Country Music Hall of Fame and Museum and the Museum of Popular Culture contribute to such undertakings, and how their curatorial practices leverage each city's musical heritages. This section considers these factors in light of the institutions' histories, the financial and material support provided by the music industry and prominent musicians (and/or their estates) featured in their exhibits, and the curatorial approaches to select exhibits staged between April 2018 and the time of writing, being July 2021.

4.1   Nashville, Country Music, and the Country Music Hall of Fame and Museum

Established in 1967, The Country Music Hall of Fame and Museum hosts a range of permanent and temporary exhibits showcasing the history and evolution of country music both within and beyond Nashville. The museum, which was first located in the Music Row neighborhood, relocated to its current downtown Nashville location in 2001. In doing so it increased in size, and in 2014, underwent further expansions to more than double its footprint to 350,000 square feet (CMHOFM, 2020a). It has received considerable support from the country music industry both within and beyond Nashville. Financial support for its 2014 expansion for example included a USD2.5 million pledge from the Academy of Country Music, and a USD4 million endowment by country singer Taylor Swift led to the establishment of the onsite Taylor Swift Educational Center (Coleman, 2013; Freeman, 2012). In addition, many other country musicians, or their estates, have donated memorabilia for display, or funds to have wings named in their honor. The museum also plays a vital role in music education, offering a range of school tours and excursions, online educational resources and hosts a series of family and community focused programs. It also operates the reissue label CMF Records and CMF Press (CMHOFM, 2020a), and the building also houses the Hatch Print Show, country music archives, and a range of theatres and performance spaces.

Country music history is showcased in the museum in relation to specific artists, sub-genres, and time-periods. The museum's core exhibition *Sing me back home: A journey through country music* presents the history and origins of country music and is complemented by range of temporary exhibits, which while building on this history demonstrates the continued relevance, success, and legacy of country music. In April 2018, for example, the *Loretta Lynn: Blue Kentucky Girl, Tim McGraw & Faith Hill: Mississippi Woman, Louisiana Man*, and *Shania Twain: Rock this country* exhibits were on display. More recently, the museum has hosted exhibits such as the *Outlaws and Armadillos: Country's Roaring 70's*—which explored the connections between the country music scenes in Nashville and Austin—and since 2019, has hosted the *American Currents: State of Music* exhibit, which reflects on key developments and successes of the genre in the preceding year (CMHOFM, 2018, 2020b). Ephemera and artefacts on display include stage costumes, handwritten lyrics, photographs (both of a personal and professional nature), screenplays, and music awards relevant to the artist, genre, and/or time period being featured. In addition, personal artifacts such as wedding dresses and documentations of marriage proposals (in the case of Tim McGraw and Faith Hill) were also on display. The museum also displays a range of musical instruments—with a particular focus on guitars given country music's guitar-centric nature—as well as replicas of notable recording studios and guitar repair workshops, such as that previously owned by Buddy Guy. Many displays are also interactive and/or include audio-visual elements such as listening and viewing stations of live performance footage and in-studio recordings.

4.2 Seattle, Grunge, and the Museum of Popular Culture

The Museum of Popular Culture (commonly known as MoPOP) was established as the Experience Music Project in 2000. Located in the Uptown Arts District, the museum underwent various name changes before settling on its present name in 2016 (Schlosser, 2016). The museum engages a wide variety of popular culture and associated fandoms across a diverse set of exhibitions which encompass film, gaming, and music. Exhibits explore key movements, events, and works of note relevant to their specific artforms with the museum also engaging in a range of educational programs, public talks, and talent competitions throughout the year (MoPOP, 2020a). While the museum engages with a broad remit of popular culture it is primarily associated music. This results from its strong focus on music in its curatorial practices (approximately one third of its displays are music-focused), its original name and focus on rock n roll music, as well as the design of the building, which drew inspiration from spliced together guitars (Dudzik & Reed, 2018; Schlosser, 2016).

Music is incorporated in the Museum of Popular Culture's exhibits across a range of exhibitions and offerings. Two notable music-focused exhibits on display in April 2018 *Wild blue angel: Hendrix abroad, 1966–1970*—a retrospective of blues guitarist and Seattle native, Jimi Hendrix at the height of this fame, as well as the *Nirvana: Taking Punk to the Masses* exhibit (with both remaining on display as of July 2024). In addition, a *Guitar gallery* is on display tracing the history of the instrument, its role in popular music culture and associated musicians. The museum also has a *Sound Lab*, an interactive display of instruments, audio technology, DJ consoles, and recording studios. More recently the museum has also played host to the *Pearl Jam: Home and Away* exhibit which traces the history of the band (MoPOP, 2021). Memorabilia featuring these exhibits includes clothing (both from stage performances and notable photo shoots), instruments, stage props, and personal and professional photographs, oral histories, short-form documentary screenings, and music listening stations.

5 Discussion

A combination of their curatorial practices, the ephemera on display, and the interactive nature of their exhibits allow the Country Music Hall of Fame and Museum and the Museum of Popular Culture to make significant contributions to the preservation and perpetuation of the genre- and place-specific country and grunge music heritages of Nashville and Seattle. This is further supported through their locations in these cities—sitting within entertainment districts (Nashville) or clusters of other related institutions (Seattle)—as well as the leveraging of their place-specific music heritages in their offerings. Despite similarities to the ways in which they engage with these genre- and place-specific heritages, there are key differences in their capacities to do so, and in turn, their contributions to the music tourism which occurs in their cities. This relates to the ways in which each city has leveraged this heritage in official tourism campaigns, and the scale and scope of their relevant music industrial complexes.

As a result of the ways in which these institutions sit within the remit of other cultural institutions within their city, the scale at which country music is memorialized in Nashville is much more prominent than the ways in which grunge is memorialized in Seattle. This is further influenced by the present-day nature of country music activity in Nashville, which is home to a thriving, internationally recognized country music industrial complex which makes considerable economic contributions to the city. Nashville's music sector contributed USD5.5 billion to Nashville's economy in 2015 alone (Harper et al., 2015). In addition, the Country Music Hall of Fame and Museum sits within a music-centric neighborhood and, through partnerships with other places of significance, such as RCA Studio B, is able to engage strongly across a range of other music tourism sites. This is further supported by the City of Nashville itself, which has capitalized on a combination of heritage and present-day music activity in its "Music City" branding and associated "Visit Music City" campaign. In addition, the Music City Total Access Pass (sold by the city's tourism office) provides pass holders with fixed cost entrance to a range of music attractions.

In comparison the Museum of Popular Culture is located within a cluster of arts, education, and science focused institutions, with its remit being broader than simply music. Therefore, while it showcases broad engagement with popular music, exhibitions which capitalize on its local music heritage, such as the *Nirvana: Taking Punk to the Masses, and Pearl Jam:*

112   C. BALLICO

Home and Away, are much narrower in their temporal scope. Where Nashville's country music history dates back nearly a century, for example, Seattle's grunge history is concentrated on activity occurring between a relatively narrow time period, being the late 1980s and 1990s. As such, the standing legacy of grunge is not as overt, nor currently active in the same way as country music is in Nashville. Arguably the difference between the two cities is a matter of both the scale and scope of their present-day music industrial complexes, and the intersection between heritage and present-day activity captured in the museum and other music-related tourism activities. Furthermore, where much of Nashville's audience-engaged country music tourism heritage centered downtown (with the exception of the Grand Ole Opry House which is located approximately 12.5 miles out of the downtown area), Seattle's grunge music history is spread out across the city and inhabiting more suburban areas. To this end, where music fans in Nashville can easily learn about and navigate the history of country music across a range of sites concentrated on the downtown Nashville area (which are also within a few blocks of one another), in Seattle, key sites of grunge history are much more spread out across the downtown area and beyond (see Figs. 5.1 and 5.2 for an illustration of this). In addition, grunge's history has not been leveraged in Seattle in the same way as Nashville's country music has in relation to the official tourism activities of the city. This is curious given that Seattle is home to a dedicated film and music office which otherwise recognizes the role the city has played in the development and sustention of global contemporary music activity. The city is also home to a thriving local music sector, which as recently as 2008 (the most recently available data) generated USD1.2 billion in sales, and USD487 in earnings. It was also credited with creating 11,155 jobs and 2618 associated businesses (OFM, n.d.).

6   CONCLUSION

In conclusion, this chapter has examined the role of the Country Music Hall of Fame and Museum and the Museum of Popular Culture in the preservation and perpetuation of place- and genre-based country and grunge music heritage in Nashville and Seattle. As this chapter has explored, the curatorial practices of these two institutions demonstrate the varying ways—and scales—to which music heritage can be leveraged within museums. In turn, through the recognition of each city's rich genre-specific music heritages, these institutions demonstrate both the key role of "place" in music tourism and how "place" can be leveraged within museum curatorial practices. In turn, the location of these two museums within clusters of related activities—be it within a remit of a downtown entertainment district and/or other music-related institutions—supports their capacity to contribute dynamic music tourism experiences in their relative cities.

REFERENCES

Atlas Obscura. (n.d.). The Fillmore East. *Atlas Obscura*. https://www.atlasobscura.com/places/the-fillmore-east-new-york-new-york

Baker, S., Istvandity, L., & Nowak, R. (2016). The sound of music heritage: Curating popular music in music museums and exhibitions. *International Journal of Heritage Studies, 22*(1), 70–81.

Baker, S., Istvandity, L., & Nowak, R. (2018). Curatorial practice in popular music museums: An emerging typology of structuring concepts. *European Journal of Cultural Studies, 23*(3), 434–453. https://doi.org/10.1177/13675 49418761796

Ballico, C., & Watson, A. (2020). *Music cities: Evaluating a global cultural policy concept*. Singapore: Palgrave-Macmillan.

Bennett, A., & Rogers, I. (2016). Popular Music Scenes and Cultural Memory UK London: Palgrave Macmillan.

British Broadcasting Corporation (BBC). (2016). Punk protest: Sex Pistols manager's son sets fire to collection. *British Broadcasting Corporation*. https://www.bbc.com/news/uk-38120496

Bulut, S. (2016). Viv Albertine defaces punk exhibition for ignoring women. *Dazed Digital*. https://www.dazeddigital.com/music/article/32077/1/viv-albertine-defaces-punk-exhibition-for-ignoring-women

Coleman, M. (2013). https://www.rollingstone.com/music/music-country/taylor-swift-opens-education-center-at-country-music-hall-of-fame-79432/

Connell, J., & Gibson, C. (2003). *Sound tracks, popular music, identity and place*. Routledge.

Cooke, P., & Huggins, R. (2004). A tale of two clusters: High technology industries in Cambridge. *International Journal of Networking and Virtual Organisations, 2*(2), 112–132.

Country Music Hall of Fame and Museum (CMHOFM). (2018). Oulaws and Armadillos: Country music's roaring 70's. *Country Music Hall of Fame and Museum*. https://countrymusichalloffame.org/exhibit/outlaws-armadillos-countrys-roaring-70s/

Country Music Hall of Fame and Museum (CMHOFM). (2020a). About us. *Country Music Hall of Fame and Museum.* https://countrymusichalloffame. org/about/

Country Music Hall of Fame and Museum (CMHOFM). (2020b). Now open: American currents: State of the music. *Country Music Hall of Fame and Museum.* https://countrymusichalloffame.org/exhibit/americancurrents/

Country Music Hall of Fame and Museum (CMHOFM). (2020c). Record-breaking attendance at the Country Music Hall of Fame and Museum in 2019. *Country Music Hall of Fame and Museum.* https://countrymusichalloffame. org/press-release/record-breaking-attendance-set-at-the-country-music-hall-of-fame-and-museum-in-2019/

Dudzik, B., & Reed, N. (2018). *Exploring visitor perceptions: Examining what visitors to MoPOP think about pop culture.* Prepared for the Museum of Popular Culture by UW Museum Evaluation Team. University of Washington.

Fairchild, C. (2017). Understanding the exhibitionary characteristics of popular music museums. *Museum and Society, 15*(1), 87–99.

Fairchild, C. (2018). Transcendent myths, mundane objects: Setting the material scene in rock, soul, and country museums. *International Journal of Heritage Studies, 24*(5), 477–490.

Farago, J. (2015). To return or not to return? *BBC.* https://www.bbc.com/culture/article/20150421-who-should-own-indigenous-art

Freeman. (2012). ACM pledges $2.5 million to HoF capital campaign. *Music Row.* https://musicrow.com/2012/07/acm-pledges-2-5-million-to-hof-capital-campaign/

Friedlander, E. (2018). *A walking tour of Manhattan's Rock 'n' Roll past: The 2000s.* Retrieved June 19, 2019, from https://www.nytimes.com/2018/11/20/arts/music/indie-rock-walking-tour-manhattan.html

Giblin, J., Ramos, I., & Grout, N. (2019). Dismantling the master's house: Thoughts on representing empire and decolonising museums and public spaces in practice an introduction. *Third Text.* 3(4–5), 471–486.

Gibson, C., & Connell, J. (2005). *Music and tourism: On the road again* (Vol. 19). Channel View Publications.

Greene, A. (2021). Rock & Roll Hall of Fame Chief Curator Nwaka Onwusa – Future 25. *Rolling Stone.* https://www.rollingstone.com/pro/features/nwaka-onwusa-rock-hall-future-25-1179542/?-roll-hall-of-fame-chief-cura

Harper, G., Cotton, C., Zimmer, C., & Scholer, R. (2015). *Culture here: A report on cultural assets and activities, Nashville assessment 2015.* Nashville Area Chamber of Commerce.

Historic RCA Studio B (HRCASB). (2020). Tours. *RCA Studio B.* https://studiob.org/plan-your-visit/tours/

Hodak, B. (2015). The real-life impact of ABC's Nashville. *Forbes.* https://www.forbes.com/sites/brittanyhodak/2015/10/28/the-real-life-impact-of-abcs-nashville/?sh=705361b01e2d

Hunt, T. (2019). https://www.theguardian.com/culture/2019/jun/29/should-museums-return-their-colonial-artefacts

Internet Movie Database (IMDB). (n.d.). Nashville. *Internet Movie Database.* https://www.imdb.com/title/tt2281375/

Johansson, O. (2010). Form, function, and the making of music-themed entertainment districts in Nashville and Memphis. *Material Culture, 42,* 47–69.

Leonard, M. (2007). Constructing histories through material culture: Popular music, museums and collecting. *Popular Music History, 2*(2), 147–167.

Leonard, M. (2010). Exhibiting popular music: Museum audiences, inclusion and social history. *Journal of New Music Research, 39*(2), 171–181.

Leonard, M. (2018). *Representing popular music histories and heritage in museums* (pp. 261–270). Routledge.

Museum of Popular Culture (MoPOP). (2017). MoPOP: 2016 Report to our community. *Museum of Popular Culture.*

Museum of Popular Culture (MoPOP). (2018). MoPOP: 2017 Report to our community. *Museum of Popular Culture.*

Museum of Popular Culture (MoPOP) (2019). MoPOP: 2018 Report to our community. *Museum of Popular Culture.*

Museum of Popular Culture (MoPOP). (2020a). Museum of Popular Culture. *Museum of Popular Culture.* https://www.mopop.org/

Museum of Popular Culture (MoPOP). (2020b). MoPOP: 2019 Report to our community. *Museum of Popular Culture.*

Museum of Popular Culture (MoPOP). (2021). Current exhibits at MoPop. *Museum of Popular Culture.* http://www.mopop.org/exhibitions-plus-events/exhibitions/

Office of Film and Music (OFM). (n.d.). Economic impact study. *Office of Film and Music.* https://www.seattle.gov/filmandmusic/music/economic-impact-study

Opry. (2021). Opry membership. *Opry.* https://www.opry.com/about-old/membership/

Pirrie Adams, K. (2015). No two houses of the holy: Creating cultural heritage in Nirvana: Taking punk to the masses. *Popular Music History, 10*(2), 113–137.

Reynolds, S. (2011). *Retromania: Pop Culture's Addiction to Its Own Past.* New York: Faber and Faber.

Ryman Auditorium. (2021). Grand Ole Opry. *Ryman Auditorium.* https://ryman.com/history/opry/

116   C. BALLICO

Schlosser, K. (2016). Meet MoPOP: Paul Allen's EMP Museum changes name to Museum of Pop Culture. *Geek Wire*. https://www.geekwire.com/2016/meet-MoPOP-paul-allens-emp-museum-changes-name-museum-pop-culture/

Seattle Centre. (n.d.). About. *Seattle Centre*. http://www.seattlecenter.com/about

Shoenberger, E. (2020). What does it mean to decolonize a museum? *Museum Next*. https://www.museumnext.com/article/what-does-it-mean-to-decolonize-a-museum/

Terrill, A., Hogarth, D., Clement, A., & Francis, R. (2015). Mastering of a music city. *Music Canada*.

Tsjeng, Z. (2020). Fundamentally, it's a question of empathy: Why Britain needs to return its colonial artefacts. *Vogue*. https://www.vogue.co.uk/arts-and-lifestyle/article/should-british-museums-return-colonial-artefacts

Whiting, C. (2021). Take a Seattle Grunge tour. *Visit Seattle*. https://visitseattle.org/things-to-do/arts-culture/music-and-concerts/take-a-seattle-grunge-tour/

CHAPTER 6

The Hidden Music City: The Role of Music Tourism Imaginaries in the Regeneration of Detroit

Leonieke Bolderman

Abstract In this chapter, the potential for as well as the hindrances to a future for Detroit as music tourism city are explored through the conceptual lens of music city mythologies: globally circulating imaginaries that connect music to place. The case of Detroit offers interesting venues for analysis as an ethnically diverse city, with music heritage and music scenes relating to different roots: which stories are being told, who makes these choices, and how does it shape the story of the city? A discussion of the function of mythologies in music tourism development is complemented with an analysis of the role of music in Detroit's current regeneration and applied to two case studies: the efforts to preserve the Grande Ballroom, where legends such as Iggy Pop and Pink Floyd performed, and the success of Movement festival, a yearly techno music festival. The case studies are based on media analysis and ethnographic fieldwork involving

---

L. Bolderman (✉)
Faculty of Spatial Sciences, University of Groningen,
Groningen, The Netherlands
e-mail: s.l.bolderman@rug.nl

© The Author(s), under exclusive license to Springer Nature
Singapore Pte Ltd. 2024
S. Guillard et al. (eds.), *New Geographies of Music 2*, Geographies of
Media, https://doi.org/10.1007/978-981-97-2072-9_6

117

118   L. BOLDERMAN

observations and interviews. By comparing policy developments in the city with these case studies, this chapter shows how music heritage and live music scenes shape the stories of the city, offering routes to both division and belonging for the local communities involved. Providing nuance to the current academic debate on the music cities framework, it is argued that who and what drives music tourism development, what policy instruments are effective, and what strategy is best (bottom up or top down), is influenced by the imaginaries and mythologies that shape the tourism geography of the contemporary music city.

Keywords Music tourism • Music cities • Urban regeneration • Detroit • Urban imaginaries • Music mythologies

1   INTRODUCTION

Detroit bows on a rich musical heritage, which includes the birth of not one but two music genres—Motown in the 1960s, techno in the late 1980s—and many world-famous artists and bands such as Aretha Franklin, J Dilla, Madonna, Eminem, Kid Rock, Aaliyah, and The White Stripes. At the same time, Detroit as the city of Fordism has become one of the symbols of urban decay (Doucet, 2017): as the city continuously tries to navigate the consequences of a changing industrial and social environment, its population fell dramatically from 1.8 million in the 1950s to around 670,000 in 2019 (US Census Bureau, 2020), resulting in mass ruination of its housing stock, the city even declaring bankruptcy in 2013 as the largest US municipality to do so in the country's history. These events have led to globally circulating images and stories of the city as urban prairie, a ghost town (Zebracki et al., 2019), making Detroit a "metonym of urban failure" (Doucet, 2017).

Bringing together these images of the city, Detroit's music industry could play a vital role in the efforts towards regeneration. Following in the footsteps of "superstar cities" such as Liverpool, Nashville, and New Orleans, this idea connects with a growing trend towards developing music cities: cities in which "music is recognized by urban policy makers for its legacy and heritage, its ability to contribute to the cultural and creative identity of the city and as a driver for tourism and for economic growth" (Ballico & Watson, 2020a, p. 3). The music cities framework connects directly to the creative cities perspective (Homan, 2014) and is especially applicable to post-industrial cities of decline (Bennett, 2020; Cantillon et al., 2020).

Chances for developing music tourism are certainly there. The mythology of Detroit's music heritage does not only exist in the minds of fans all over the world, in circulated mediated images, and in narratives of the sounds of the city. It is also present materially in buildings such as the Fox Theatre and Baker's Keyboard Lounge (claiming to be the oldest operating jazz club in the world); it is memorialized in the guided tours of heritage organization Preservation Detroit; it is brought back to live through exhibits in local museums such as the Motown Museum; while it is also visible in the music murals scattered across the city (Bolderman, 2024). Besides these heritage-related locations that could facilitate music tourism, the city also has some attractive festivals such as Movement Electronic Music Festival, Detroit Jazz Festival, and Mo Pop Festival.

However, in spite of its musical potential and in spite of the current moment for music city development, Detroit is not mentioned when superstar music cities are discussed. In this chapter, the potential for as well as the pitfalls and hindrances to a future for Detroit as music tourism city are explored. Recognizing and highlighting the importance of mythologies and imaginaries in the development of music cities and music-related tourism, this chapter argues that Detroit's status as a hidden music city stems from the conflicting imaginaries and social tensions around its redevelopment.

The case of Detroit offers interesting venues for analysis, since it is an ethnically diverse city, with music heritage relating to different roots: which stories are being told, who makes these choices, and how does it shape the story of the city? A discussion of the function of mythologization in music tourism development is complemented with an analysis of the role of music in Detroit's redevelopment and applied to two case studies: the efforts to preserve the Grande Ballroom, the famous venue where legends such as Iggy Pop and the MC5 performed, and the success of Movement Electronic Music Festival, a techno music festival taking over Downtown Detroit each year during Memorial Day Weekend. The case studies are based on media analysis, field observations, and a range of informal interviews, forming the initial stage of a research project on the role of Detroit's various music scenes and music heritage in its regeneration. The research was undertaken between July 2017 and July 2020, a period during which the author lived and worked in Detroit 6 months out of each year. By comparing policy developments in the city with the two case studies, this chapter shows how music heritage and live music scenes shape the stories of the city. Providing nuance to the current academic debate on the music cities framework, it is argued that who and what drives music tourism development, and what policy instruments and strategies are effective, is influenced by the imaginaries and mythologies that shape the tourism geography of the contemporary music city.

2   Music Tourism Development: Processes of Mythologization

Music tourism can be defined broadly as the phenomenon of people traveling because of a connection with music (Bolderman, 2020, p. 2; Gibson & Connell, 2005). In recent years, music tourism has developed from a grassroots pursuit with some eye-catching successful examples such as tourism to Elvis' Graceland and Beatles tourism to Liverpool, into a steady niche in the global tourism landscape (Bolderman, 2020). Music tourism can have a considerable impact on local communities, places, and people. A recent development is the rise of music cities: cities that focus their branding and marketing strategies on their music heritage and live music scenes, utilizing music-focused branding to stimulate tourism flows, in the hopes of serving as accelerator of economic development and urban regeneration. This development is visible not only in policy decisions, but also in the existence of the UNESCO City of Music designation established in 2006 as part of the creative cities network, the rise of consultancies such as Sound Diplomacy, the release of practitioner reports such as "The Mastering of a Music City" by IFPI/Music Canada (2015) with strategies on how to create and develop a music city brand, and the emergence of a body of academic work on the music cities phenomenon, such as exemplified for example by A. Baker (2019), Ballico and Watson (2020b), Holt and Wergin (2013), and Homan (2014).

Looking at music tourism development, a central role and driver of music tourism is the process of circulating imaginaries that connect music to place (Bolderman, 2020), resulting in the mythologization of place through music (Bennett, 2002; Gibson & Connell, 2005). Tourism as a phenomenon in general is based on the circulation, appropriation, and activation of the imagination, as destinations trigger the imagination of the tourist in a hermeneutic process of meaning making (Urry & Larsen,

2011). Salazar (2012) calls these understandings of destinations tourism imaginaries: "socially transmitted representational assemblages that interact with people's personal imaginings and are used as meaning-making and world-shaping devices" (Salazar, 2012, p. 864). As argued by Bolderman in recent work on music tourism, music-related tourism imaginaries, or "musical mythscapes," are central to tourist experiences of music tourism, influencing all phases of tourist experience (Bolderman, 2020). Imagining places influences the stage before travel, as music listeners create affective ties to their imagined destination (Bolderman, 2020; Bolderman & Reijnders, 2019), and this affective connection plays a key role in experiencing a music tourism location on site (Bolderman, 2020; Bolderman & Reijnders, 2017). After having stepped into the musical mythscape, the tourist returns home where the mythscape is adjusted and reinscribed with the experience (Bolderman, 2020).

Whereas this conceptualization of musical mythscapes is focused on the experiences of the tourist, it is by no means a process that excludes the role of locality. Music can play a particularly seductive role in informing understandings and expectations of particular places (Bennett, 2002; Bolderman, 2020, 2024), as the relation between music and place is intimately connected to images and ideas of local culture and heritage (Gibson & Connell, 2005). The place-based imaginary of the sound of a city is taken up in the global circulation of mediated images, narratives, and ideas. Based on this process of mediatization, music can turn into the intangible heritage of place (Bolderman, 2020; Brandellero & Janssen, 2014; Cohen, 2007; Gibson & Connell, 2005), which in turn can be made tangible again by erecting for example museums, heritage walks, and plaques of commemoration (Baker, 2015; Brandellero & Janssen, 2014). "Superstar cities" such as New Orleans, Liverpool, and Nashville are created and are as successful as they are as music tourism cities through this process of what Ballico and Watson call "external mythologizing" (Ballico & Watson, 2020a).

In recent years a powerful economic imaginary around music and urban revitalization has surfaced, spurring music tourism development through emphasizing the economic advantages of leaning into the music mythology of a city. Bennett (2020) has described twin imaginaries at play in contemporary music cities: the City of Music imaginary and the Music City imaginary. Both imaginaries are driven by economic incentives of redevelopment and regeneration, where musical resources are a source of economic gains for a city. The City of Music imaginary is connected to the

UNESCO City of Music designation, involving a top-down public approach to music heritage as driver of urban development. The second imaginary, the Music City, focusses on an industry-led development of live music scenes to create a bustling city with exciting nightlife, music performances, and festivals to draw in the crowds, using local music for tourism and branding (Bennett, 2020, p. 20).

In the case of music, this framework especially reverberated in the context of cities of post-industrial decline (Baker et al., 2020; Ballico & Watson, 2020a; Cantillon et al., 2020; Holt & Wergin, 2013), music having the ability to bring liveliness, and in its wake, visitor streams, back to derelict city centers. Especially in the UK this tactic created successful example cities, such as Liverpool and Birmingham, and it is why many cities have tried to copy their success in adopting culture-led redevelopment plans and projects (Quinn, 2010).

However, the focus on art and culture for urban redevelopment has come under criticism, especially because the economic, social, and cultural impacts are not unequivocally positive. For example, Richard Florida's thesis on the creative class (Florida, 2017) offers a one-size fits all solution to post-industrial decline, in which creating an attractive city for the creative class will also stimulate tourism. As has been pointed out by others, this global strategy excludes local specificity, ignoring the path dependency of cities (for example Scott, 2008), and the characteristics of local development that can have either stimulating or detrimental effects on urban development.

In the case of music tourism, as has been pointed out by O'Meara and Tretter (2013) through a case study of music tourism development in Austin, a singular focus on a certain kind of music and music tourism can exacerbate racial inequality and social tension. In Austin, the focus of live music in city marketing and the tourism offer on (white) rock and country music excluded grassroots, more diverse local music scenes. In contrast, recognizing both the issues and potentials of music tourism development for struggling cities, both Bennett (2020) and Baker et al. (2020) point out that a more bottom-up, localized approach, involving local heritage and local communities, can actually contribute to local wellbeing and place attachment, a dimension of music city development that could positively contribute to urban development for post-industrial cities.

In this chapter, I will explore these issues surrounding music tourism development in the contemporary music city through the lens of music mythologies, applied to the case study of Detroit. Detroit has a rich musical heritage that is heavily involved in mediatized processes of mythologization: Motown and techno are genres that speak to the imagination of global audiences, while Detroit's famous artists live in the imagination of fans across the world. However, Detroit is not a "superstar music city" on the same level as New Orleans, New York, Liverpool, and Nashville. In the next sections, I will explore the role of culture-led policy development in the current situation of the city and will apply this general history to two case studies, involving the issues surrounding music heritage preservation and live music scenes in the city.

3   Detroit Music Heritage in Urban Policy

The city of Detroit government focused explicitly on music, entertainment, and sports as tools for redeveloping the dilapidated downtown area in the period between 1994 and 2007 (Che, 2008). Before this time, Detroit had seen decades of steady decline from its heyday as the "Paris of Northern America" in the early twentieth century (Galster, 2014; Sugrue, 2014). Detroit had made its fortune as the quintessential city of Fordism, automobile production creating favorable conditions for economic development (Galster, 2014). The city grew exponentially, and by the 1950s had grown to around 1.8 million inhabitants. However, due to processes of suburbanization and "white flight", deindustrialization and racial tensions, the city started losing inhabitants rapidly, while further economic decline resulted in a city in despair by the 1980s (Sugrue, 2014). An attempt was made to reverse the fortunes of the downtown area and lure back office workers by stimulating mega projects such as the General Motors Renaissance Center at the Detroit Riverfront in the 1970s, a strategy headed by Detroit's first black mayor Coleman Young. This did not help Detroit much, and the decline of the city continued in a rapid pace (Galster, 2014), eventually culminating in municipal bankruptcy in 2013.

Deborah Che has analyzed the role of music and other art forms in Detroit city policy up until the early 2000s (Che, 2007, 2008, 2009, 2012). With mayors Archer (1994–2001) and Bing (2001–2007), Detroit adopted the economic imaginary of redevelopment through culture and, in the case of Detroit, sports and entertainment (Che, 2008). The focus was on stimulating redevelopment of the downtown area through public-private partnerships, from which the rest of the city was expected to profit, in line with creative city theory—Richard Florida was part of the advisory committee to the city (Che, 2008). Three major casinos were built, and in the early 2000s the process of relocating all major sports stadiums from their suburban locations back to downtown was completed. The focus initially was on creating an entertainment district around the sports stadiums, the Foxtown area, in a public-private collaboration involving the influential local Ilitch family, who made their fortune with the Little Caesar's pizza chain. The Foxtown area was expected to have theatre, bars, and nightlife, creating a bustling downtown.

As part of the focus on sports and nightlife, the city stimulated plans to attract mega events to the city, for example the Superbowl in 2006 (Che, 2008). Stimulating and offering grants for music festivals also became part of the strategy, most notably the free Detroit Jazz festival that had already started in the 1980s, and the Detroit Electronic Music Festival that was organized for the first time in 2000, the forerunner of what now is Movement Electronic Music Festival ("Movement", Che, 2012). Both the actual economic impact and the impact on the image of Detroit of the building frenzy and the eventification of the downtown area, which was one of the main marketing drivers for the plans, were not immediately clear (Che, 2008). Even so, in her analyses Che was still optimistic about the opportunities these strategies offered for redeveloping the struggling city at the time of writing at the end of the 2000s (Che, 2007, 2008, 2009, 2012).

With the economic crisis of 2008, Detroit entered a next phase of urban decline, spurring an international image of a city in ruin (Zebracki et al., 2019). Under force of economic hardship, the strategy of the city changed, in that there was little funding for redevelopment available, and the city planning program focused even more on public-private partnerships, a strategy that was written down in the Detroit Works Project and its 2012 Detroit Future City Framework Plan (Clement & Kanai, 2015; Fraser, 2018; Zebracki et al., 2019). These plans shifted the focus away from music, entertainment, and sports as drivers of downtown development, as the attention of the city officials needed to shift to rezoning and resizing the city areas outside of the downtown area. Dan Gilbert, the Detroit-based owner of Quicken Loans, had started to buy and redevelop property downtown, moving his company headquarters to central downtown, and investing heavily in revamping the city core. In turn, city hall turned attention to other areas of the city in dire need of action: the "empty spaces" of urban decline and ruin that were marring its reputation (Clement & Kanai, 2015; Fraser, 2018).

6 THE HIDDEN MUSIC CITY: THE ROLE OF MUSIC TOURISM IMAGINARIES… 125

As described by Clement and Kanai (2015) and Fraser (2018), Detroit Future City ("DFC") put forward several imaginaries of its own: an imaginary of urban prairie, being emptied of ruins and ready for innovation and pioneering, by investors who would see its potential. An imaginary of urban greening as well, making space for urban farms and greening initiatives. As the research by Clement and Kanai (2015) and Fraser (2018) delves into, with these imaginaries the ideal of redevelopment aimed to attract young, adventurous inhabitants, with a pioneering spirit, to populate the "uninhabited" land (Clement & Kanai, 2015; Fraser, 2018; Zebracki et al., 2019). However, these areas were not unpopulated and so the plans raised protest, since it would remove and replace the poor, and predominantly black communities who actually stayed in place throughout Detroit's hardships (Fraser, 2018), in favor of replacing them with young, often white, urban professionals (Clement & Kanai, 2015), showing the power of urban imaginaries to shape the lifeworld of the local communities involved.

In the Detroit Future City plans, the emphasis was on improving basic city functions such as infrastructure, dealing with the many empty buildings in the city, and starting a reversal of the tendency of middle-class inhabitants to relocate to the suburbs (Detroit Works Project Long-Term Planning Steering Committee & Detroit Future City, 2013, p. 9).[1] In the framework document, art is mentioned in a more general sense, as part of neighborhood regeneration "through fusion of art and industry" (DFC, 2013, p. 56), with one of the goals to "incorporate local arts into comprehensive public space master plans" (DFC, 2013, p. 57). In the introduction to the plan, among Detroit's assets is stated that the city boasts "the second largest theater district in the country, second only to New York City" (DFC, 2013, p. 9). Music is only mentioned explicitly in reference to Detroit's role in music industry development: "Detroit's assets also include the resiliency, creativity, and ingenuity of its people and organizations—the city's human and social capital. Detroit's impressive talent base includes business leaders who forever changed the culture of industrial production and music (…)" (DFC, 2013, p. 9).

Reading the DFC documents, in contrast to the years between 1994 and 2007 analyzed by Che, music is not presented as a central asset in its proposed development strategies, nor does it seem to play a role as central marketing theme for the city. Where the focus on dealing with immediate

---

[1] Shortened to "DFC" for further references.

issues such as ruination, crumbling infrastructure, and a low tax base might explain the shift of focus, it does not become clear from the documents itself why art and specifically music are seen as considerable assets, but were not put into the forefront of the development plans more. Looking at the imaginaries presented, the role of the empty land image described in the urban prairie and urban greening imaginaries perhaps does not fit naturally with the idea of a rich musical heritage and vibrant live music scene already present in these areas.

After the bankruptcy and the public criticism on the DFC plans, most activity engaging with Detroit's musical heritage and live music scenes was in private and corporate hands. For example, Dan Gilbert's development company Rock Ventures emphasizes that stimulating the nightlife economy is a goal for redeveloping downtown in their tours of company offices and the downtown projects they are developing, creating an exciting city life and interesting events for the returning young professionals, "who want to have something to do if they are moving into the newly converted lofts and industrial apartment buildings" (tour guide Rock ventures tour, 1 May 2019). Rock Ventures is involved in organizing and supporting events in the central Campus Martius area, Hart Plaza and Riverfront, all located downtown, while it also sponsors the Detroit Jazz Festival through Gilbert's company Quicken Loans, as a result of which the festival has remained free of charge. Besides Rock Ventures, private initiatives in the city include for example the preservation efforts of the Vanity and the Grande Ballrooms, and the work of the Detroit Sound Conservancy, campaigning to preserve the Blue Bird Inn Jazz club.

In a most recent turn of events, and topic of more extensive research for this project in the future, the municipality seems to have re-embraced the power of art and culture for city regeneration. Beautification is a strategy of the city, as it supports and invests in murals projects across town to beautify less attractive areas close to downtown that are very slowly starting to gentrify under the success of public-private investment, such as Midtown, Eastern Market, and the Corktown and Mexicantown areas (Bolderman, 2024). The municipality supports for example the Murals in the Market festival and the Detroit Walls project, which in public-private partnerships counter blight, and aim to stimulate local community involvement (Bolderman, 2024). In February 2020, a new Office of Arts, Culture and Entrepreneurship was announced. In the announcement, Detroit's lack of attention to its cultural heritage and the role of arts and culture in the city is explicitly referred to—the creative city imaginary at play (*Office of Arts, Culture and Entrepreneurship*, 2020, p. 1):

> Here in Detroit, we sometimes forget how great we are! Detroit is a mecca with music, murals and magnificence. Detroit is a repository for art, design, and architecture. We are the birthplace of Motown Records and techno (thank you Juan Atkins, Kevin Saunderson and Derrick May). And we helped elevate hip-hop, rap, rock and jazz. We offer the world the Detroit International Jazz Festival, which brought 320,000 music-lovers downtown last year and the three-day Movement Electronic Music Festival, where 25,000 fans a day celebrate the Motor City as the birthplace of techno.

As the pamphlet further adheres to, and the image that rises from this brief discussion of the role of music in Detroit's policy development, is that municipal policy is shaped by a kaleidoscopic, decentralized approach to its art and culture industries and tourism development. The consequences of this situation for the potential of music heritage and live music scenes to contribute to Detroit's regeneration will be discussed in more depth in the next two sections, focused on Detroit techno and Movement Festival, and the preservation efforts of the Grande Ballroom.

4   DETROIT MUSIC CITY: THE POTENTIAL OF TECHNO

Techno music has its roots in Detroit, and as discussed above has been the subject of a music city imaginary as possible driver of tourism and thereby economic development. As briefly highlighted above, Movement Electronic Music Festival ("Movement") has been especially central to this idea for the municipality. Movement started out as the free Detroit Electronic Music Festival in the year 2000, organized by event producer Carol Marvin through her company Pop Culture Media, with techno legend Carl Craig as artistic director (Burns, 2010; Che, 2012), supported by a grant and favorable permits from the city mayor's office. In an oral history of the festival compiled by Resident Advisor (Burns, 2010), Phil Talbert, the special activities coordinator of the Detroit Parks and Recreation Department in 2000, explains how the municipal support for the festival was inspired by the image building capacity of a techno music event:

We needed to get the mayor, Dennis Archer, up to speed on what electronic music was, and what this festival could mean. [Because we thought] it might help how the city was viewed in the United States and abroad. We thought that if we made an investment in showing that this could happen, that the city was safe, that it would be a help in bringing a new demographic to the city of Detroit. We felt we could do that through electronic music, if we did it right…There was some fear there though. We didn't want to do something that could be negative for the city.

The festival changed hands and names the next two years, being organized by other big Detroit techno names Kevin Saunderson and Juan Atkins respectively. It remained free of charge due to Ford sponsorship and private investment by the organizers, since the grant from the municipality was discontinued. The festival became Movement Electronic Music Festival in 2006, after event organizers Paxahau Events negotiated with the city for permission to use the dates and the location (Burns, 2010).

Looking at media coverage of the festival in local and national press, the power of techno music to attract particular audiences is portrayed to have positive spillover effects in generating revenue for local businesses and hotels, and in providing attractive amenities for longer term residents to the area—in line with the Music City imaginary as described by Bennett (2020). A 2015 article in *Forbes Magazine* for example focusses on the economic benefits of Movement, citing Sam Fotias, Paxahau's Vice President of Operations (Robehmed, 2015):

There are no financial impact figures for festival, since such studies would need to be undertaken by state bureaucracy—a hard ask of a city whose coffers are empty. But organizers believe it's making a difference. Said Fotias: "We have a huge impact with restaurants and gigantic impact with hotels, taxis and Ubers." And: "What we have is a huge tourism generator for the city," (…) "Because of the history of the music here, it's always been a pilgrimage of sorts for people to come from all over the world.

In coverage of the 10-year anniversary of the festival in 2016, the demographic the festival attracts was highlighted across articles, especially in local news outlets such as The Detroit Free Press. The festival is emphasized to attract 24- to 35-year-olds predominantly, gathering techno fans both locally and from afar (Sundius, 2016), playing into the demographic that is a driver for urban redevelopment: the young urban professional.

6 THE HIDDEN MUSIC CITY: THE ROLE OF MUSIC TOURISM IMAGINARIES... 129

A returning image evoked is that of the festival being a symbol of hope for the struggling city. A quote by DJ and producer Kirk Degiorgio summarizes this (Burns, 2010):

> There was a guy there with his whole family, and he literally was in shock. He was saying, "I never thought I'd see the day when people in Detroit would gather in such numbers to an event like this. For my family to experience this celebration of their city is overwhelming." I still remember that conversation, and it really struck me how important the festival is to that city. That might get lost now in that there are so many festivals all over the world. It means a whole lot more to a city like Detroit than just a regular festival.

The importance of the festival, as can be deduced from this quote, is presented to lie in stimulating a positive image of Detroit, as opposed to its identity of a city in ruin. What this quote shows as well is how economic imaginaries are bound up in ideas and images of the city, they are "embedded in webs of meaning that are historically situated in particular localities and social attachments" (Bennett, 2020, p. 23). Here the idea of music mythologies comes into play, as music creates especially powerful images of place identity. Rob Theakston, interviewed for the same Resident Advisor piece, echoes a similar sentiment: "Every day I read something like, Detroit's a ghost town, it's Baghdad, hell on earth whatever. But every time I go back home it's like God, there's so many great things going on" (Burns, 2010). In a quote by German techno insider Mario Husten in the Detroit Free Press the power of music mythologies comes through as well: "One thing Detroiters need to do is buy into the romantic view of the city that so many Europeans have (…). To them it isn't a backwater, but a mysterious promised land that has created most of the music they love" (Zlatopolsky, n.d.)

Husten is part of Detroit-Berlin Connection, an initiative from Berlin-based techno industry members to help Detroit develop its techno heritage and leverage its potential. Driven by Tresor-founder Dimitri Hegemann, "the Detroit-Berlin Connection is a collaborative, transatlantic effort to bring together creative individuals and communities in the two cities with the goal of driving cultural and economic growth in Detroit" (www.berlindetroit.de). Plans were made to help Detroit become a "new Berlin," since Berlin has been successful in creating opportunity and leverage its techno image for development, attracting for example "techno tourists" (Garcia, 2016). One of the ideas of Detroit-Berlin connection was to create a club in the former Packard Automotive Plant, one of the famous ruins of Detroit bought up by a project developer (Hucal, 2018). Another plan was to convert the Fisher Body Plant 21, another huge industrial ruin, into a 100-bed hostel and club (Zlatopolsky, n.d.). According to Hegemann: "In any empty building I see an opportunity—and there are so many opportunities in Detroit" (Hucal, 2018). In these words, an echo of the urban prairie imagery voiced by Fraser (Fraser, 2018) can be read—an endless, boundless space of opportunity that is ready to be made profitable by the pioneers daring to dream and do.

However, as with the urban prairie imagery that Fraser responded to, the Detroit techno landscape was not empty either. In talking with several local DJ's and venue visitors, some doubts about the Detroit-Berlin plans are voiced about the sustainability of such a large venue for the Detroit techno audience year-round: "Movement is great for the city, everywhere you look is techno, but I wonder if there is an audience big enough to make that club viable all year long in the long term" (Local DJ, 2 May 2019). This point connects with an issue that is present in music city development in general: the tension between focusing on events versus investing in a local infrastructure of venues to sustain the scene throughout the year (Ballico & Watson, 2020b; Mommaas, 2004).

This concern also chimes in with the criticism on Detroit's dispersed music infrastructure, voiced in an essay by local journalist and blues guitarist Keith Owen on ways Detroit can become what he calls a "Music Capital": "despite our indisputable musical legacy, which spans three generations on both the national and international scenes, it's sometimes difficult to hear on street level. There is no central music district where visitors and tourists can go to sample the best of what we have to offer" (Owens, 2015). Indeed, Detroit does not have a music district similar to Beale Street in Memphis or French Quarter in New Orleans. Detroit's famous music district Paradise Valley was demolished during the 1960s to make way for two freeways, and since then nothing resembling an area that is dedicated to and promoted by the city as a music district has replaced it. There were plans to develop a new music district after the Foxtown sports stadiums development (Che, 2008), but the issues of a government in decline, lack of funding, and a lack of corporate-private initiative to take the place of government support have meant these plans were stalled.

Another concern voiced is a familiar issue with stimulating nightlife for urban development: the issue of permits and noise control. This issue is not only brought up in the interviews, but also stated in the media analyzed and recognized by Hegemann himself (Zlatopolsky, n.d.): state and municipal legislation forbids a club to be open all night long, as is characteristic of successful techno clubs like Tresor in Berlin. In line with the way Ballico and Watson define the success of music cities (Ballico & Watson, 2020b), a music city is more than a successful scene; it needs the infrastructure to support it. In the case of Detroit, the practical infrastructure of permits stands in the way of the characteristics of what is a desired experience for clubbers, while the spread-out nature of the city and its existing music venues does not deliver an immediate eyecatcher for tourists.

Since its announcement in 2018, the plans of the project developer have stalled on the redevelopment of the Packard Plant ruin, and the status of the Detroit-Berlin plans is unclear. What this short discussion of press coverage and interview data has revealed is that the image of a successful festival in offering opportunities for development does not (yet) meet the practical side of music city development. Moreover, there is an overlap in urban prairie imagery that has been pointed out to play into social and racial inequalities, glossing over the residents and local developments that are (still) in place in areas of ruin.

5 Detroit City of Music: Preserving the Grande Ballroom

The second imaginary identified by Bennett (2020) in his discussion of music and urban development is the City of Music imaginary: the role of top-down heritage designations and policies in creating attractive places to visit for tourists and locals alike. Detroit's lack of attention towards its music heritage is lamented in several articles and as described by the municipality's office of Art, Music and Entrepreneurship itself. One of the ways this lack of interest in its own heritage is visible is in the ways the preservation of built music heritage is handled. As discussed in the policy overview, heritage preservation in Detroit is left to private initiative. One of the organizations that is investing in Detroit's music heritage is Detroit Sound Conservancy, for example in protecting the site of the Blue Bird Inn, a famous Detroit Jazz club (Cantillon et al., 2020). Besides Detroit Sound Conservancy, conservation efforts are driven by private individuals,

132   L. BOLDERMAN

such as in the case of the Grande Ballroom. This example offers a rich case to explore how economic music imaginaries pervade not only the work of top-down governmental and bottom-up industry initiatives, but private support and protection of music heritage as well.

The Grande Ballroom was one of Detroit's most iconic rock music venues throughout the 1960s, hosting the Stooges, Led Zeppelin, Velvet Underground, Pink Floyd, and the MC5 (Early & Gibb, 2016). The building currently is owned by a church congregation, the Chapel Hill Missionary Baptist Church, and is in a ruinous state. Led by a local historian, a group called "Friends of the Grande Ballroom" has undertaken several initiatives to preserve the building. The group is mainly a virtual community on Facebook, consisting of patrons, former employees of the ballroom and fans—the leader of the group himself for example never visited the Ballroom in his youth, but became a fan of the building and its history through the stories of its fame told to him by friends and family (personal communication, 19 January 2020).

The group has organized several fundraising activities that have contributed to the buildings' preservation and have increased its attraction as a destination for visitors to commemorate its history. For example, a fundraising campaign in 2017 raised money for an official assessment of the building's viability, while a 2019 campaign focused on raising money for emergency roof renovations, raising $6925 by 96 donors (Cantillon et al., 2020). Most notable from a tourism point of view, the group has also commissioned a mural in collaboration with Wayne Kramer, a former bandmember of the MC5. The mural depicts Wayne Kramer in his MC5 heyday, during the time the band had its short but eponymous career play out mainly in this venue (Bolderman, 2024). The mural depicts Kramer playing his guitar, shooting stars, stripes and flowers across the wall, a white panther figuring at the other side of the mural. The mural hereby references both the music and legend of the band and the hall it is painted on, while also referencing the bands' involvement in the white panther movement (Early & Gibb, 2016). The mural was finished in 2018, and, according to Kramer and the Friends of the Ballroom, already attracts tourists and fans coming to see what is left of the building (personal communication, 20 June 2019).

The preservation of the building could, like other popular music heritage projects, potentially contribute to community wellbeing (Baker et al., 2020), playing into the way Music City imaginaries tend to emphasize "music's civic or social value in improving well-being and contributing to

6 THE HIDDEN MUSIC CITY: THE ROLE OF MUSIC TOURISM IMAGINARIES... 133

social cohesion" (Bennett, 2020, p. 20). Baker et al. point out three ways in which that goal can be reached: by involving communities that connect people, by engaging or mobilizing vernacular histories and memories, and by focusing on heritage narratives that connect people with places. Through the grassroots, bottom-up approach of the Friends of the Ballroom, these three conditions seem to be met: the fundraising activities connect people across online spaces; generating and building on their personal stories connected to the Ballroom; connecting them with the preservation of the actual building on site. The mural specifically solves a problem familiar to Detroit in the context of postindustrial decline: through the mural, the owners of the building are not cited for graffiti charges and blight anymore, and the mural in this sense adds to the beautification efforts of the city in creating more attractive spaces for visitors to enjoy the rougher edges of the city. In this sense, the Ballroom as an initiative to save the building and turn it into a destination for fans and tourists alike, supported by private initiative and funding, is a good example of battling some of the issues of top-down heritage preservation initiatives driven by government support, as has also been pointed out by Cantillon et al. (2020).

However, a closer look at the communities involved does show a level of tension present in the Ballroom preservation efforts. As in the case with the marketing efforts of Austin described by O'Meara and Tretter (2013), the preservation of the Ballroom has a racial dimension that erases certain heritage narratives in favor of others. This tension is clearly felt in the discussion I had when visiting the Ballroom in the company of two Friends of the Ballroom. They talked about the complex relation with the congregation, exemplified for instance by the initial refusal of the congregation to support the historical designation of the building with the local government. This necessitated the Friends to reapply for the designation and delaying preservation initiatives such as the building integrity report.

One of the reasons the two Friends thought the congregation was not too happy with the work of the Friends is the history of the Ballroom. In its heyday, the venue attracted patrons from the wealthy white suburbs, who would cause traffic issues for the predominantly black neighborhood. The historical tensions between the patrons and the local community carry over to today, since the Friends of the Ballroom group consists mainly of people not local to the still predominantly black neighborhood. One of the Friends for example explained that he lives in Dearborn, a city close to Detroit that the local black community has contentious feelings with due to a long history of segregation and racism, which according to the Friend has impacted their collaboration with the church congregation: "I cannot say for certain, but it has not helped that I live in Dearborn. It took me a long time to get the pastor to trust me, and even now I have issues with dealing with the congregation because of who I am, where I live and what that represents" (Friend 1, January 19, 2020). Unfortunately, the difficulty experienced by the Friends carried over into this research project, since it has not been possible (yet) to get into contact with members of the congregation themselves to discuss their point of view on these matters.

At the moment of research, in the ideas of the Friends the main purpose of the building would be a place of worship and reflection, in line with the interests and needs of the owner, the congregation. The Friends would lead the renovation of the building, and would like to run a small museum inside the building that would commemorate its music history. However, besides the complex relation with the owner, the Friends suffer from a lack of consistent funding to realize their plans for the building. What does not help this situation is that the Friends are not an official charitable organization; a charitable 501c3 tax status allows for any donations to be tax deductible, and is needed to receive grants. As it stands, the future of the preservation and of turning the venue into a tourism destination is uncertain.

The case of the Grande Ballroom thereby shows various difficulties in private development of music heritage for tourism and regeneration purposes, in spite of its potential in a postindustrial development perspective. The Music City imaginary is present in the ideas to make the Ballroom as music heritage visible and visitable for tourists, the mural fitting in with beautification efforts aimed to lessen the burden of urban ruins while it also offers an instagrammable sight for tourists. However, the story of the role of the venue in its neighborhood, and the interest of the congregation to use the venue for worship purposes, potentially stands in conflict with the imaginary played into by the group of volunteers interested in its redevelopment.

6 Conclusion

Movement Festival and the efforts to preserve the Grande Ballroom show the potential of music heritage and live music scenes for developing tourism and thereby the regeneration of the city; however, these examples also bring to light the complex issues associated with stimulating arts and culture as tools of urban development. Movement especially shows the tension between investing in yearly mega events versus developing an infrastructure for a local music scene that is capable of attracting audiences year-round. The Grande Ballroom case shows how private initiative is not enough to develop a successful tourism attraction, as well as the tensions caused by social inequality and racial disparities that complicate the preservation of the iconic building even further—whose heritage is represented and preserved, whose stories are told, and who should be its guardians?

Through these practical and social issues, Detroit shows how various imaginaries and mythologies are at odds when analyzing the potential of a city for developing music tourism. Detroit as a mythological music city exists alongside Detroit as a city of modern urban ruin and high crime, even called a "metonym of urban failure" (Doucet, 2017). Its development narratives revolve around the economic imaginaries of the Music City, while more recent development plans have introduced an imaginary of greening and innovation (Fraser, 2018), in which music plays a more subordinate role as medium of an urban pioneering vibe. What the case of Detroit above all shows is how concrete issues such as who drives music tourism development and what policy instruments and investment strategies help or hinder successful music city marketing is influenced strongly by the imaginaries and mythologies of a city that are emphasized through these more practical and concrete issues, revealing whose stories of development are told, and whose are silenced.

REFERENCES

Baker, S. (2015). *Preserving popular music heritage: Do-it-yourself, Do-it-together*. Taylor and Francis.

Baker, A. (2019). *The great music city: Exploring music, space and identity*. Palgrave Macmillan.

Baker, S., Nowak, R., Long, P., Collins, J., & Cantillon, Z. (2020). Community well-being, post-industrial music cities and the turn to popular music heritage. In C. Ballico & A. Watson (Eds.), *Music cities. Evaluating a global cultural policy concept* (pp. 43–62). Palgrave Macmillan.

Ballico, C., & Watson, A. (2020a). Introduction. In C. Ballico & A. Watson (Eds.), *Music cities. Evaluating a global cultural policy concept* (pp. 1–19). Palgrave Macmillan.

136   L. BOLDERMAN

Ballico, C., & Watson, A. (Eds.). (2020b). *Music cities: Evaluating a global cultural policy concept*. Palgrave Macmillan.

Bennett, A. (2002). Music, media and urban mythscapes: A study of the 'Canterbury Sound'. *Media, Culture & Society, 24*(1), 87–100. https://doi.org/10.1177/016344370202400105

Bennett, T. (2020). Re-rewind: Heritage, representation and music city aspiration in Southampton. In C. Ballico & A. Watson (Eds.), *Music cities. Evaluating a global cultural policy concept* (pp. 19–42). Palgrave Macmillan.

Bolderman, L. (2020). *Contemporary music tourism: A theory of musical topophilia*. Routledge.

Bolderman, L. (2024). #Detroit music city: Analyzing Detroit's musical urban imaginary through a cultural justice lens. *Space and Culture, 27*(1), 14–30.

Bolderman, L., & Reijnders, S. (2017). Have you found what you're looking for? Analysing tourist experiences of Wagner's Bayreuth, ABBA's Stockholm and U2's Dublin. *Tourist Studies, 17*(2), 164–181. https://doi.org/10.1177/1468797616665757

Bolderman, L., & Reijnders, S. (2019). Sharing songs on Hirakata Square: On playlists and place attachment in contemporary music listening. *European Journal of Cultural Studies.* https://doi.org/10.1177/1367549419847110

Brandellero, A., & Janssen, S. (2014). Popular music as cultural heritage: Scoping out the field of practice. *International Journal of Heritage Studies, 20*(3), 224–240. https://doi.org/10.1080/13527258.2013.779294

Burns, T. L. (2010, May 18). Put your hands up: An oral history of Detroit's electronic music festival. *Resident Advisor.* https://ra.co/features/1186

Cantillon, Z., Baker, S., & Nowak, R. (2020). A cultural justice approach to popular music heritage in deindustrialising cities. *International Journal of Heritage Studies*, 1–17. https://doi.org/10.1080/13527258.2020.1768579

Che, D. (2007). Connecting the dots to urban revitalization with the Heidelberg Project. *Material Culture, 39*(1), 33–49.

Che, D. (2008). Sports, music, entertainment and the destination branding of post-Fordist Detroit. *Tourism Recreation Research, 33*(2), 195–206.

Che, D. (2009). Techno: Music and entrepreneurship in post-Fordist Detroit. In O. Johansson & T. L. Bell (Eds.), *Sound, society and the geography of popular music* (pp. 261–280). Ashgate.

Che, D. (2012). Building the beloved community through techno music production in Detroit. In B. Warf (Ed.), *Encounters and engagements between economic and cultural geography* (pp. 123–141). Springer.

Clement, D., & Kanai, M. (2015). The Detroit future city: How pervasive neoliberal urbanism exacerbates racialized spatial injustice. *American Behavioral Scientist, 59*(3), 369–385. https://doi.org/10.1177/0002764214550306

Cohen, S. (2007). *Decline, renewal and the city in popular music culture: Beyond the beatles*. Ashgate.

6 THE HIDDEN MUSIC CITY: THE ROLE OF MUSIC TOURISM IMAGINARIES... 137

Detroit Works Project Long-Term Planning Steering Committee & Detroit Future City. (2013). *Detroit future city: 2012 Detroit strategic framework plan.* https://detroitfuturecity.com/strategic-framework/

Doucet, B. (2017). *Why Detroit matters: Decline, renewal, and hope in a divided city.* Polity Press.

Early, L., & Gibb, R. (2016). *The Grande Ballroom: Detroit's rock "n" roll palace.* The History Press.

Florida, R. L. (2017). *The new urban crisis: How our cities are increasing inequality, deepening segregation, and failing the middle class – And what we can do about it.* Basic Books.

Fraser, E. (2018). Unbecoming place: Urban imaginaries in transition in Detroit. *Cultural Geographies, 25*(3), 441–458. https://doi.org/10.1177/1474474017748508

Galster, G. (2014). *Driving Detroit: The quest for respect in the motor city.* University of Pennsylvania.

Garcia, L.-M. (2016). Techno-tourism and post-industrial neo-romanticism in Berlins electronic dance music scenes. *Tourist Studies, 16*(3), 276–295. https://doi.org/10.1177/1468797615618037

Gibson, C., & Connell, J. (2005). *Music and tourism: On the road again.* Channel View Publications.

Holt, F., & Wergin, C. (Eds.). (2013). *Musical performance and the changing city. Post-industrial contexts in Europe and the United States.* Routledge.

Homan, S. (2014). Liveability and creativity: The case for Melbourne music precincts. *City, Culture and Society, 5,* 149–155.

Hucal, S. (2018, June 1). A Berlin club owner's mission to give back to Detroit, the city that gave Europe techno. *ABC News.* https://abcnews.go.com/International/berlin-club-owners-mission-give-back-detroit-city/story?id=55583750

IFPI & Music Canada. (2015). *The mastering of a music city: Key elements, effective strategies and why it's worth pursuing.* IFPI and Music Canada.

Mommaas, H. (2004). Cultural clusters and the post-industrial city: Towards the remapping of urban cultural policy. *Urban Studies, 41*(3), 507–532. https://doi.org/10.1080/0042098042000178663

O'Meara, C. P., & Tretter, E. M. (2013). Sounding Austin: Live music, race, and the selling of a city. In F. Holt & C. Wergin (Eds.), *Musical performance and the changing city. Post-industrial contexts in Europe and the United States* (pp. 52–76). Routledge.

Office of Arts, Culture and Entrepreneurship. (2020). https://detroitmi.gov/news/mayor-duggan-rochelle-riley-lay-out-vision-citys-ace-office

Owens, K. (2015, March 17). 13 ways Detroit can assert itself as a music capital. *Model D Media.* https://www.modeldmedia.com/features/detroitmusiccapital031715.aspx

138   L. BOLDERMAN

Quinn, B. (2010). Arts festivals, urban tourism and cultural policy. *Journal of Policy Research in Tourism, Leisure and Events, 2*(3), 264–279. https://doi. org/10.1080/19407963.2010.512207

Robehmed, N. (2015, August 24). How Detroit is monetizing techno. *Forbes.* https://www.forbes.com/sites/natalierobehmed/2015/08/24/how-detroit-is-monetizing-techno/?sh=4829ad3a12b5

Salazar, N. B. (2012). Tourism imaginaries: A conceptual approach. *Annals of Tourism Research, 39*(2), 863–882. https://doi.org/10.1016/j.annals.2011. 10.004

Scott, A. J. (2008). *Social economy of the metropolis: Cognitive-cultural capitalism and the global resurgence of cities.* Oxford University Press.

Sugrue, T. J. (2014). *Origins of the urban crisis: Race and inequality in postwar Detroit.* https://doi.org/10.1515/9781400851218

Sundius, M. (2016, May 24). Paxahau's Jason Huvaere talks Kraftwerk & Techno tourism for movement festival's 10-year anniversary. *Billboard.* https://www. billboard.com/articles/news/dance/7385047/paxahaus-jason-huvaere-talks-kraftwerk-techno-tourism-for-movement

United States Census Bureau. (2020). Detroit City, Michigan. Retrieved from: https://data.census.gov/profile/Detroit_city,_Michigan?g=160 XX00US2622000

Urry, J., & Larsen, J. (2011). *The tourist gaze 3.0* (3rd ed.).

Zebracki, M., Doucet, B., & De Brant, T. (2019). Beyond picturesque decay: Detroit and the photographic sites of confrontation between media and residents. *Space and Culture, 22*(4), 489–508. https://doi.org/10.1177/1206331217753344

Zlatopolsky, A. (n.d.). Berlin techno entrepreneur continues to eye Detroit site. *Detroit Free Press.* Retrieved July 29, 2021, from https://eu.freep.com/story/entertainment/music/2015/04/16/dimitri-hegemann-detroit-berlin-tresor/25900439/

INDEX[1]

A

Aesthetics, 22–24, 29–32, 38, 40–41, 47, 49n3, 50, 78, 81
Album, 9, 10
Anthropology, 5
Appropriation, 13, 24, 28, 29n3, 35, 40–41, 57, 78, 120
Audience, 29, 33, 34n8, 83, 90, 100, 102, 105, 123, 128, 130, 135
Authenticity, 6, 10, 13, 27, 32, 34, 35n9, 40, 51, 67, 90, 91, 103

B

Bars, 10, 30–32, 49, 80, 81, 83, 84, 86, 86n7, 105, 124
  See also Clubs; Venues
Black, 12, 38, 123, 125, 133
Branding, 47, 104, 111, 120, 122
  See also Marketing
Buenos Aires (Argentina), 9, 14, 74–94

C

Caribbean, 30, 30n5, 36–38, 36n10
Centrality, 6, 46
Circulation, 5, 93, 120, 121
Clubs, 10, 11, 49, 119, 126, 130, 131
  See also Bars; Venues
Clusters, 98, 104, 107, 111, 113
  See also Districts
Cocoa Beach (United States), 12, 13, 22–28, 30–34, 36–40, 42
Compact Discs (CDs), 79
Concerts, 10, 23, 27, 31–37, 40, 41, 47, 49, 56, 57, 59, 60, 79, 80, 85, 87, 89, 90, 92
  See also Performance; Shows
Consumption (of music), 3, 37, 40
Country (music), 30, 40, 104–112, 122
Creative cities, 5, 10, 119, 120, 123, 127
Creative class, 122
Creative economy, 4

---

[1] Note: Page numbers followed by 'n' refer to notes.

© The Author(s), under exclusive license to Springer Nature Singapore Pte Ltd. 2024
S. Guillard et al. (eds.), *New Geographies of Music 2*, Geographies of Media, https://doi.org/10.1007/978-981-97-2072-9

139

140   INDEX

Creativity, 5, 12, 27, 28, 47, 50, 56, 67, 125
Cultural economy, 40, 41

D
Dance, 14, 29n3, 74–87, 89, 91, 93
Detroit (United States), 15, 99, 118–135
Diffusion, 3, 10, 12–14, 77
Digital technology, 5, 63
Discourse, 8, 30, 40, 85, 101
Disk jockeys (DJs), 77, 79–80, 110, 129, 130
Districts, 15, 77, 78, 80, 84, 98, 99, 104, 106, 111, 113, 124, 125, 130
    See also Clusters
Downtown, 11, 15, 26, 27, 98, 99, 101, 105, 106, 108, 109, 112, 113, 123, 124, 126, 127

E
Ecology (of music), 6
Ethnography (Internet and digital), 51
Eventification, 13, 47–51, 61, 63, 65, 66, 124
Experience, 3, 9, 10, 13, 14, 23, 27, 28, 32n7, 33, 35–38, 41, 47, 48, 53, 60, 62, 63, 67, 79, 90, 91, 93, 103, 113, 121, 129, 131

F
Fans, 10, 11, 100, 107, 112, 119, 123, 127, 128, 132, 133
Festivalization, 13, 46–47, 51, 66
Festivals, 10, 11, 47, 60, 62–64, 75, 77, 79, 80, 83, 87, 89, 90, 92, 93, 101, 102, 119, 122, 124, 126–129, 131

G
Gender, 6
Genre, 6, 9, 11, 12, 14, 15, 23, 29, 30, 30n6, 36–40, 50, 60, 77, 78, 82, 82n6, 89, 98, 99, 103, 104, 107, 109, 118, 123
Gentrification, 47, 100
Globalization, 3, 76, 91
Glocal, 36–40
Golden age, 14, 77, 78, 80–82, 86, 93
Government (local), 87, 133
Grunge, 14, 98–113

H
Hall of Fame, 98, 99, 104–106, 108–112
    See also Museum
Heritage, 8, 9, 11–15, 30, 74–94, 98–113, 118–127, 129, 131–135
History (of music), 12
Hybridization, 6–8, 39

I
Identity, 11, 22–24, 28, 31, 32, 39–41, 60, 75, 78, 83, 85, 86, 104, 118, 129
Imaginaries, 5, 6, 9, 10, 15, 74, 80, 118–135
Inequality, 12, 122, 131, 135
Infrastructure, 11, 35, 40, 104, 107, 125, 126, 130, 131, 135
Innovation, 25, 27, 59, 87, 125, 135
Interdisciplinary, 2–15
Interviews, 23, 77, 81n4, 85, 86, 91–93, 119, 131

J
Jerram, Luke, 13, 48–53, 49n3, 56–58, 60–67

INDEX   141

L

Lifestyle, 13, 22–29, 31–33, 35n9, 36, 36n10, 37, 39, 63
Lyrics, 3, 4, 10, 37, 74, 83, 84, 93, 102, 109

M

Marketing, 32, 76, 83, 120, 122, 124, 125, 133, 135
  See also Branding
Media, 5, 6, 24n2, 27, 29, 50, 66, 102, 119, 128, 131
Milonga, 14, 75, 77–82, 89, 90, 92, 93
Mobility, 4, 75–77, 88–91, 93, 94
Montevideo (Uruguay), 74
Mp3, 79
Museum, 12, 14, 15, 47, 75, 77, 83–85, 93, 98–113, 119, 121, 134
  See also Hall of Fame
Music cities, 11, 13, 15, 103, 104, 111, 118–122, 127, 128, 130–132, 134, 135
Musicians, 5, 9, 14, 33, 60, 75–94, 81n5, 100–103, 105, 108–110
Music industry, 3, 5, 6, 23, 78, 103, 108, 109, 118, 125
Musicking, 23, 23n1, 29, 30, 36, 41
Musicology, 5, 7
Mythology, 15, 22, 119–122, 129, 135

N

Nashville (United States), 14
Nature, 4–6, 25, 34, 39, 49, 85, 99, 102, 104, 109–111, 131

Neighborhoods, 11, 12, 47, 107, 109, 111, 125, 133, 134
Networks, 5, 7, 10, 41, 74, 89, 92, 120
New York City (United States), 48, 58, 125
Nightlife, 122, 124, 126, 131
Noise, 31, 35, 40, 131
Nostalgia, 9, 10, 77–79, 100, 102, 103

P

Paris (France), 14, 76, 77, 79, 88, 89, 91–93, 123
Participant, 23–25, 33, 35n9, 36, 57, 59
Participant observation, 23, 36
Performance, 12, 13, 22, 23n1, 33, 38, 49, 51, 56, 57, 60–62, 65, 74, 80, 80n3, 81, 101, 102, 104, 105, 109, 110, 122
  See also Concerts; Shows
Piano (street), 13, 46–67
Place-making, 8–15
Place-specific, 40, 98, 99, 103–107, 111
Policy, 5, 7, 9, 11–15, 46–48, 60, 61, 63, 66, 76, 82–88, 93, 118, 120, 123–127, 131, 135
Popular music, 2–15, 30n6, 37, 98–108, 110, 111, 132
Power, 34, 35, 53, 58, 67, 125, 126, 128, 129
Preserve, 11, 82, 87, 98, 99, 119, 126, 132, 134
Production (of music), 3, 5, 6, 12, 25, 50, 75

142 INDEX

Public space, 13, 24, 31–36, 38, 48, 52, 56, 57, 61, 62, 77, 125
Punk (music), 29, 30, 100

R
Race, 6
Radio, 38, 50, 77, 104, 107
Recording, 33, 82, 87, 100, 102, 104, 110
Regeneration, 12, 15, 46, 60, 118–135
See also Revitalization
Reggae (music), 29, 30, 30n5, 36–40
Region, 25, 27–30, 30n5, 32, 47
Repertoire, 14, 50, 80–82, 86, 89, 92
Representation, 3, 9, 24, 25, 37, 41, 56, 78, 102, 103
Reputation, 25, 83, 90, 124
Revenue, 12, 128
Revitalization, 47, 48, 52, 56, 60, 121
See also Regeneration
Rock (music), 29, 30, 36, 38, 40, 50, 78, 82, 110, 122, 127, 132

S
Scale, 35n9, 40, 47, 58, 64, 66, 67, 76, 88, 93, 100, 104, 107, 108, 111, 112
Scene, 6, 7, 9–15, 22, 30n6, 31, 37, 39, 40, 75, 79, 81, 90, 92, 99, 102–104, 106, 107, 109, 119, 120, 122, 123, 126, 127, 130, 131, 134, 135
Seattle (United States), 14, 15, 98–113

Shows, 10, 11, 15, 28, 29, 53, 61, 65, 75, 77–80, 83, 84, 86, 89–93, 99, 106, 120, 129, 133–135
See also Concerts, Performance
Sociology, 5
Songs, 3, 5, 9, 10, 31, 74, 80, 84, 85, 102, 104, 107
Sound, 2–4, 7, 10, 23, 27, 30–36, 38, 40, 50, 102, 106, 119, 121
Soundscape, 2, 13, 23, 28, 31, 36–41, 77, 91
Sound Tracks, 3
South
    region, 28
    United States, 24
Spatiality, 2–15
Stakeholders, 11, 48, 52, 57–59, 63, 66
Street, 13, 33–35, 49, 50, 52, 53, 58, 61, 62, 64, 81, 84, 130
Styles, 3, 11, 66, 81, 87, 89, 92
Subcultures, 22–42
Suburbs, 78n1, 81, 92, 125, 133
Sun Bum, 22, 23, 26–28, 32, 32n7, 33, 35, 35n9, 36, 38–41
Surf, 12, 13, 22–33, 30n5, 35–41
Surfanization, 22, 24, 41, 42

T
Tango, 9, 11, 14, 74–94
Techno (music), 118, 119, 123, 127–131
Territory, 4, 36, 75, 83
Theatres, 63, 109, 124
Theory, 4, 7, 123
Touring, 48, 49, 64, 66, 67

INDEX   143

Tourism, 7–15, 24, 25, 28, 31, 47, 75,
    80n3, 83–85, 88, 93, 98, 99,
    101, 103–113, 118–135
Translocal, 12, 75, 91
Transnational, 10, 39, 74–94
Travel, 121

U
UNESCO, 82, 88
United States (US), 14, 24, 25, 29,
    38, 118, 128
Urban development, 23, 78, 83, 122,
    131, 135

Urban geography, 5, 9, 23
Urban space, 9, 12–15, 22, 23, 25–27,
    36, 39, 41, 47, 53, 65, 74

V
Value, 10, 25, 33, 37, 38, 67, 90,
    102, 132
Venues, 15, 49, 52, 56, 59n6,
    60–62, 75, 77–81, 90,
    92, 100, 104, 105, 107,
    119, 130–134
    See also Bars, Clubs
Vinyl records, 79, 88

Printed and bound by CPI Group (UK) Ltd, Croydon, CR0 4YY
03/12/2024
01799311-0010